Thank you for the privilege of reading the manuscript of your forthcoming book...

I could feel the warmth of your heart in reading this manuscript. Your keen understanding and sense of compassion for the pastors you have known reminds me of the tender love I see in a mother for her children.

I finished the manuscript with the thought that I wished somewhere in their educational pilgrimage, you could have taught each of my children.

This book could be a healing ointment for pastors who have been wounded by conflicts and hostile experiences in their ministry. It is more than a manual — it is a tender expression of appreciation for those who endeavor to minister to the spiritual life of those whom they seek to serve.

The affirmation of your faith — "These I Believe" — is a clear and positive foundation for what you have written in the book. It is the song of a healthy spiritual soul that has been baptized in the deep and sometimes painful experiences of life.

It is a book that could not only be helpful and encouraging to pastors, but its greatest potential might be to foster in laypeople a better understanding and appreciation of their pastor.

Sincerely,
W. Burkette Raper

Dr. Raper is President Emeritus of Mount Olive College, Mount Olive, North Carolina. He devoted fifty years to the college — forty-one years as President and nine years as Director of Planned Giving.

T0143732

Thank you for the opportunity you gave me to read your most interesting manuscript. As I reviewed it, I knew that it truly came from the heart. It is a beautiful testimony of your journey of faith which you now share with others. Much of what you have shared is a reflection of your Christian faith and how your spirit has been touched and you have grown as a result of knowing many Christian leaders.

You did an excellent job in providing some very practical information and insights into a journey of faith. These are practical tips for Christian leaders. Any church leader would be blessed and enriched by reading this work...

Thank you again for allowing me to read your inspiring book. I was truly blessed by the experience.

Sincerely,
Opey D. Jeanes

Dr. Jeanes is Vice President of Special Services, Mount Olive College, Mount Olive, North Carolina.

I wish to thank you for the honor of reviewing your text. The privilege is above measure.

You have an exquisite gift for communicating your feelings, thoughts, and experiences without cluttering the material with unnecessary jargon – making your book a delight to read.

I found this particular text to be quite astute and helpful. You convey the message of the book with elegance and practicality, which will make this work a tool not only for the church, but also for the minister.

Please accept my view suggestions as you will. By no means am I an expert. Once again, thank you for this honor.

Yours in Christ,
Otis Hamm

Pastor Hamm, Saratoga Free Will Baptist Church, Saratoga, North Carolina, continues his post-graduate studies in theology at Campbell University, Buies Creek, North Carolina. He contributed the chapter entitled "The Call to the Ministry."

A VIEW FROM THE PEW

A TRIBUTE TO
PASTORS

including
"These I Believe"
Affirmations of Faith

Joyce Proctor Beaman

New York

A View From The Pew
A Tribute to Pastors

by Joyce Proctor Beaman

Biblical quotations from the King James Version

ISBN 978-1-60037-359-6 (Paperback)
ISBN 1-933596-78-3 (Hardcover)

Published by

MORGAN · JAMES
THE ENTREPRENEURIAL PUBLISHER ™
www.morganjamespublishing.com

Morgan James Publishing, LLC
1225 Franklin Ave. Ste 325
Garden City, NY 11530-1693
Toll Free 800-485-4943
www.MorganJamesPublishing.com

Habitat
for Humanity®
Peninsula
Building Partner

Cover and interior design by
Bonnie Bushman
bbushman@bresnan.net

Acknowledgments

I wish to thank the following who so willingly read the manuscript and sent encouraging responses: The Reverend Otis Hamm, current pastor of the Saratoga FWB Church (NC); Dr. Opey D. Jeanes, Mount Olive College (NC) Vice President for Special Services; Tommy Manning, former editor of the Free Will Baptist Foundation, Ayden (NC); Dr. Dalton R. Proctor, my brother, and former director of 4-H, state of North Carolina; Dr. W. Burkette Raper, President Emeritus, Mount Olive College (NC); The Reverend Julius Whitley, current pastor of Good News Advent Christian Church, Saratoga (NC). (Even though these persons helped immeasurably, they bear no responsibility for the contents and syntax of this book.)

Also, many thanks to the Reverend Otis Hamm, my current pastor, for contributing information for the chapter entitled "The Call." At the time of this publishing, Pastor Hamm was pursuing a Master of Divinity at Campbell University, Buies Creek (NC). Appreciation, too, to the Reverend Julius Whitley and his wife, Starr, neighbors, for the idea, *A View from the Pew*; and to Marci R. Rollins-Smart, editorial assistant, Free Will Baptist Press, Ayden (NC) for researching and preparing the extensive list of references for ministers and others. (These references are in a chapter entitled "Reference Books to Consider.") At the time of publishing, Marci was pursuing her Master of Divinity at Campbell University, Buies Creek (NC). Also, many thanks to my brother, Robert Proctor, for his encouraging words while I was writing this book.

Many heartfelt thanks to Linda Eason Moore, friend and former student, for speaking to me about contacting Morgan James Publishing Company about the possibility of publishing this book.

As with the others, there are not words to express sufficient gratitude to those at Morgan James Publishing including David L. Hancock, founder of Morgan James Publishing, who so enthusiastically accepted my manuscript for publication and followed faithfully the publication process from beginning to end; to Cindy Sauer, administrative assistant at Morgan James Publishing, who answered countless questions along the way; to Bonnie Bushman, who worked so diligently on the layout and cover design; to Heather Kirk, author coordinator, who knew the answers concerning publishing and shared all she knew so readily and willingly; and to all other members of the Morgan James staff who worked with my manuscript. Each was so patient and professional.

I wish I could include all the names of each person — friends and kinsmen — who "walked" with me throughout the writing and publication of this book. Someone emphasized that I would surely fail to list someone, and that I would "worry forever." And so I would! But as Dr. W Burkette Raper said in the baccalaureate sermon several years ago (see chapter eleven, final paragraph), "God knows your name," and I believe He rejoices in each of you because of your love for Him, and your support of this book, a book about Him, His Son, His Holy Spirit — and the work of His followers here on earth. I am glad that we have the blessing of living on God's earth at the same time, and that He let our lives touch for Him through this book. Thank you all, each one.

Many thanks to each person who contributed ideas included in the chapters. You were so generous, helpful, and kind to share your thoughts, observations, experiences — and love! Thank you for giving me permission to use your sharings for His glory and to help and to inspire others who love Him and work in His vineyards.

DEDICATION

This book is dedicated to all the pastors
who have touched my life
throughout more-than-seven decades.

IN MEMORY OF

my father
Jesse David Proctor
1904-1987

my mother
Martha Pauline Proctor
1908-1995

and

my brother
David Owen Proctor
1936-1993

In Appreciation

To my son
Robert David Beaman
whom I call Bobby David
and to his wife
Donna Marie Beaman
for their expertise and assistance

and

to my granddaughter
Ashley Marie Beaman
whom I love immeasurably

and

to my husband
Robert Hines Beaman
whom I call Bob
for his patience and support
while I was writing this book
and the other books

OTHER BOOKS BY THE AUTHOR

Broken Acres

All for the Love of Cassie

Bloom Where You Are Planted

You Are Beautiful: You Really Are

Teaching: Pure and Simple

One Way of Looking (poetry)

TABLE OF CONTENTS

LET US
BEGIN

Chapter One

MY PRAYER AND PURPOSE

The purpose of this book is fourfold:

To express love, praise, honor, and thanksgiving to God, His Son, and His Holy Spirit

To pay tribute to my pastors who have so deeply touched my life

To provide, through these memories, thoughts and ideas inspired by these pastors

To share ideas and inspirations which have come to my own spirit

My prayer is that God, His Son, and His Holy Spirit will accept these words, and that His pastors will find ideas and inspirations to glorify His name and to help others, as many pastors have helped me.

You, as pastors, have used most, or perhaps all, of the ideas presented in this book; but I hope that reviewing them and seeing them together, in one text, will be a blessing and a worthy reference.

Chapter Two

THE BIRTH OF THIS BOOK

I have been blessed to listen to, and to work with, many pastors. Each one was an excellent role model and a devout Christian. I never experienced one word of pain, controversy, or rejection from any of them. Not one! Many of my pastors, now living, will verify this.

Even though my parents, my brothers, and I had always attended church, my mother and dad began taking my three brothers and me to a small country church near our home when I was eleven years old. Because there was no one to play the piano for Sunday school, I began playing the piano, though poorly, for Sunday school and later for church and all other services, a responsibility and a joy that lasted more than thirty-three years. (In later years, I was blessed that another pianist/organist was available from time to time.)

The thoughts and sharings of this book are gleanings from listening to pastors at that church as well as at other churches throughout the years. These pages record the thoughts, philosophies, approaches, and examples toward effectiveness, common sense, and spiritual leadership among the pastors with whom I was blessed to work and from whom I was blessed to learn.

I am sorry that I cannot give credit to individual ministers and pastors for thoughts and ideas used, but I feel that each will accept any effort from others, or me, to share, for the glory of God, whatever we have seen, heard, felt, or experienced from their voices, spirits, and faith.

No chapter consists of a sermon or any other lengthy presentation because I did not keep notes — nor do I have memory for extensive recall.

All that we have experienced has become a part of us. Many of those experiences — parts of oneself — go into the writings of those who choose to share through the written word. You will therefore find thoughts and inspirations from my own heart and spirit as you read.

I asked a minister what we, as children, could do to repay our parents. He said that there is no way to repay, that all we can do is to pass to others the love of parents and the love of God through loving and serving God with all our heart, loving and helping others all that we can, and by living the best we can in our church, work, family, community, and country.

And so it is that I pass to you what I have been blessed to hear, see, read, and experience. I hope that someday, as you stand in a holy place on this good earth to minister to God's people, that a chosen thought from pastors who are now living, or who have ministered in earlier years, will bless you and help to sustain you in the great work that you have been called to do.

Prior to this book, I had written other hardcover books. I thought I had finished writing books.

But alas! On Easter Sunday, 2003, the idea of this book came to me. That afternoon, I sat on my bed, pencil in hand, and wrote in longhand fifteen chapters. (I had written the other books in longhand also, except a few chapters of my book about public-school teaching.)

I knew that writing this book was something that I just had to do.

Though God is in the other books, written or implied, this one is special to me. I know that you understand why.

Chapter Three

MINISTER: PASTOR: PREACHER

The word *minister* has several meanings, both religious and secular. Some think of the word *minister* as representing an area of work, just as we say that someone is a teacher or lawyer. The word, with various meanings, is used over 160 times in the Bible.

We sometimes say that someone is "called into the ministry," referring, of course, to the work of a spiritual leader. Others prefer to use the words *pastor*, *preacher*, or some other term, depending on denomination and chosen faith.

Generally, dictionaries define *pastor* in two ways: as a minister or priest in charge of a church, or as a person who has spiritual care of a number of persons.

Historically, the words *shepherd* and *pastor* were synonymous. A shepherd — or pastor — protected his sheep, fed them, searched for them when they went astray, and cared for them when they were sick or injured. We remember the parable of the lost sheep (Matthew 18:12; Luke 15:4).

Shepherds were also spiritual leaders in the church.

The word *pastor* is first used in the Bible in the book of Jeremiah. Consider Jeremiah 3:15: "And I will give you pastors according to mine heart, which shall feed you with knowledge and understanding" (KJV). The New Testament includes these words: "And he gave some, apostles; some prophets; and some evangelists; and some pastors and teachers" (Ephesians 4:11 KJV). The beloved Twenty-Third Psalm begins: "The Lord is my shepherd. I shall not want" (Psalm 23:1 KJV).

John 10:14-17 records the words of Jesus: Verse 14: "I am the good shepherd, and know my sheep, and am known of mine. 15 As the

7

Father knoweth me, even so know I the Father: and I lay down my life for the sheep. 16 And other sheep have I, which are not of this fold: them also I must bring, and they shall hear my voice; and there shall be one fold and one shepherd. 17 Therefore doth my Father love me, because I lay down my life that I may take it up again" (KJV).

There are eight references to *pastor* or *pastors* in the Bible, more than twenty-five to *pasture* and *pastures*, more than sixty to *shepherd* or *shepherds*, and over 125 to *sheep*.

Another term used to refer to the ministry is the word *preacher*. In the Old Testament, Ecclesiastes begins: 1 "The words of the preacher, the Son of David, king in Jerusalem. Vanity of vanities, saith the preacher, vanity of vanities, all is vanity" (Ecclesiastes1:1-2).

Also, the word *preacher* is used in Ecclesiastes 7:27 and Ecclesiastes 12:8-10.

In the New Testament the word *preacher* is used in Romans 10:14; 1Timothy 2:7; 2 Timothy 1:11; and 2 Peter 2:5.

In sharing these pages, I shall use the words *minister, pastor,* and *preacher* interchangeably, and even at times, perhaps, choose another representative identification.

Because there is a majority of male ministers, and so that I do not need to use *he/she* each time, I have chosen the pronouns *he, his,* and *him*. I hope my choice is understood and accepted. But many praises to – and much respect for – our women ministers, always!

Chapter Four

THE PASTOR'S WIFE

A special blessing always comes with a new pastor — a pastor's wife.

Surely, every person who is called to the ministry prays that God will send — or gives praise and thanksgiving because God has already sent — a Christian wife who will walk hand-in-hand with him, not only as a wife but also as a coworker and helpmate, wherever he is called to serve.

Through the years, I have been blessed to enjoy our pastor's wife as a dear Christian friend.

Our pastor's wife attends all services and assists in all ways that she can. For example, when women are involved in an indoor baptism, our current pastor's wife assists.

She welcomes us when we visit the parsonage. We welcome her and her husband when they come to visit us at home or in the hospital. They are like family: They are family!

Over the years, a pastor's wife may have been involved in public work, as is our current pastor's wife, but she — as well as all the others — has always found time for her husband's ministry — and for us.

Always, I have been concerned about a pastor's wife because she, like other public workers, is under constant observation.

Also, often a pastor does not receive monetary compensation comparable to other professions. Of course, this affects budgeting and other decisions. A minister and his wife should be among the best paid because their work is for God and for all the people on earth. The calling is of God — and it is eternal.

Over the years, without exception, each new pastor and his wife did much observing and asking, initially. They wanted to learn the "modes and methods," as well as the dreams and concerns, of their new church family. They knew that soon they would be able to blend their talents and experiences — and their faith — with their new congregation to make an even-more-effective church.

Members of the congregations with whom I have been blessed to worship will verify that the wife of each pastor was "an angel among us." No exceptions!

Chapter Five

THE MISSION OF A PASTOR

Ask almost any child why he or she loves Jesus, and the child will give one of many answers: Because Jesus loves me. Because Mama and Daddy say that I should. Because my Sunday school teacher taught me to love Him. So I can be a good person. So I can go to Heaven when I die. So I can tell others about Jesus... These are all good, normal, reasonable, correct answers: We are saved so that we can enjoy these blessings and assurances.

In addition to those spoken by the children, our pastors give us expanded, important answers that enhance and supplement the children's beautiful responses. To summarize and share:

We are saved so that we can

> honor God, His Son, and His Holy Spirit with praise, love, reverence, and prayer

> bring honor and glory to Him with our whole being: our thoughts, actions, choices, and words

> worship Him in every way that we know

> work in His vineyard wherever and whenever He calls

> bring others to God and His Son and Holy Spirit and

> help others in any way that we can in His name.

Our pastors help us to do these through preaching, speaking, teaching, listening, counseling, and praying with us and for us; through visiting, planning, assisting, and in many other good ways, including inspiring us to listen for that still small voice (see 1 Kings 19:12). Especially, they do it all through their good life — the example that they live among those of their pastorate.

If one refers to Alexander Cruden's *Complete Concordance to the Old and New Testament*, one finds over 270 references to the word *praise*, over 170 to *worship*, over 450 to *glorify* or its forms, more than 164 to *honor*, more than 90 to *exalt*, and more than 500 to *love*.

We remember that the first four of the Ten Commandments are concerned with worshiping God (Exodus 20).

As my pastors emphasized, all the joys that we receive because we love God and try to follow Him are gifts, but the main purpose of our salvation is to praise Him and worship Him — often, always, forever — and to do all that we can to lead others to Him, His Son, and His Holy Spirit.

Chapter Six

THE CALL TO THE MINISTRY

A minister who read the original manuscript for this book suggested a chapter concerning the call to become a minister. I certainly agree. To receive the call from God must surely be the ultimate earthly gift and experience.

Ministers say that the call comes to each person in a special way. They also share that one who is called by God will surely, without doubt, recognize the call immediately — or usually, within a short time.

Because I have not received the call to the ministry, I asked my current pastor, the Reverend Otis Hamm, to write about the marvelous, miraculous experience. The following is what he wrote:

"Many books have been written regarding the "call." The call that God places on one's life to do His work is unmistakable and mysterious. It is filled with settled uncertainty and a whole range of other emotions and attributes. There are, however, three general truths concerning *vocare* — the call; the vocation:

1. One feels restless with one's present condition. Often when God is attempting to move in our lives, we find ourselves in a state of uncomfortable uncertainty. We realize that God is trying to say something to us, but we are not sure what. This can lead to a sense of fear as to what God has in mind: Will I have to move? Will I have to go back to school? Will I go to a foreign country? What will my family think? - and other similar questions.

    We find ourselves struggling with the idea of the call so much that we often lose sleep, get testy, and sometimes become rather angry because of our uncertainty.

2. One feels a tugging at the heart. This is the Holy Spirit prodding us, much in the same way He did when we first made the

commitment to ask Jesus into our lives. This is a feeling difficult to mistake. Emotions run high. We now feel a great joy in knowing that God has something to say — something for us to do — but we also find the elements of fear, self-doubt, and even denial. The tugging, however, will not go away and must be answered.

3. One feels the need for, and seeks, confirmation. This usually comes from someone inside the faith community — a pastor, Sunday school teacher, deacon, or other person close enough to be able to discern that God is moving in one's life. Everyone needs an Eli. Remember that Eli told Samuel to "go listen to the Lord and do as He said."

Pastor Hamm continues:

"Three examples of *call*:

Jesus

Jesus is our perfect example in all things. Concerning the call, I feel that the life of Jesus teaches us, among other things, that the call must be inner-directed. The Spirit of the Lord must dwell within to manifest itself beyond the confines of the heart. Also, the call involves journeying in many areas including geographic, spiritual, and intellectual, and it often comes with risks, especially economic ones.

Samuel

One has to be in place to hear God's call. This is physical, spiritual, and emotional. One needs helpers – Elis. These are the ones who provide the person called with the encouragement necessary for the journey.

Paul

Within Paul's call, evidence exists that helps even the older persons realize that God's call, among other assurances, is that they have not wasted their lives to this point. All that has been a part of their lives in the past will become useful in their future ministries.

Paul also understood the concept of growing in knowledge. He did this by preparation for his ministry, not by "jumping-in-feet-first" and finding that he was not ready."

Pastor Hamm continues: "The call is a very special aspect of our relationship with God. All Christians are called to serve God in one way or another; however, the call into a specific ministry is one which sets individuals apart to perform various ministries that God has called them to perform.

Always, one thing to remember is that callings can, and often do, change. One may be called into youth ministry for a season, and then later, the Lord may change that call to missions, the pastorate, teaching, or other areas that He desires. The key is to remain faithful, watch vigilantly, keep an open mind, and listen for the voice of God."

Chapter Seven

WHAT NEW PASTORS
DO SPONTANEOUSLY

By nature, character, and choice, new pastors do these initially and spontaneously – and we, as his congregation, do what we can to help him.

Pastors ask about

> Those who are in hospitals, rehabilitation centers, veterans' hospitals, rest homes, and similar facilities

> Those who are homebound by illness or for other reasons such as caring for an aged parent

> Those who are grieving because of the loss of a loved one

> Those who may have special concerns, including spiritual concerns, with which the pastor may help

Seeking these people early in the pastorate shows that the pastor is genuinely concerned about those of his congregation. We think of King David and his well-known lamentation: "I looked on my right hand, and beheld, but there was no man that would know me; refuge failed me; no man cared for my soul" (Psalm 142:4 KJV).

As pastors know, one of the deacons, elders, a member of the pastoral committee, or pulpit committee can help identify the people who need the pastor early in his pastorate.

In every congregation, surely there are those who no longer attend church services. A pastor uses various ways to get in touch: by letter, phone, or visit — by prayer.

The pastor and a committee can be in touch with absentees to let each member know about the new pastor and his desire that each one attend whenever possible.

A new pastor receives a church directory, if one is available, which has pictures of each member. Early in his ministry in the new church, he will soon become aware of those who cannot attend or who do not attend.

No one knows better than a pastor that a church family is a little world all its own. All kinds of people are among his flock. There are always people who need their pastor and those who are hungry for help. By a pastor's own great nature and his own great calling, he will find them. A pastor always knows that he does not walk alone: God walks with him to help His people.

The Reverend Stephen A. Smith, a former superintendent of the Children's Home at Middlesex, North Carolina, shared with our church the following:

While he was superintendent, someone asked him whether he felt that he loved all the children the same.

His answer was that he did indeed love each one with all his heart. Then he added, "But I reckon I love the one the most who needs me the most at the moment."

A pastor's spirit knows that it is not always the great sermons, but also the great services that inspire, lift, and bless. He knows that people may not remember all the words of sermons, but they will not forget the prayer, the look of concern on his face, the love in his eyes, and the touch of his hand in their time of great need.

THE WORSHIP
SERVICE

Chapter Eight

Opening Hymns of Adoration and Praise

In addition to Scripture, prayers, and the sermon or message, there are other verbal parts of worship — the Doxology, the Gloria Patri, and other hymns and anthems of adoration and praise. These are often sung in unison at the opening of the service, though they are often used throughout the service.

A choice of all my pastors, and one that seems to work very well, is an opening hymn of adoration and praise. Almost always, most of these hymns are found on the first pages of the hymnal. As you know, below the title of the hymn are listed the writer (whose name is on the left) and the composer of the music (whose name is on the right). Here are titles of hymns of adoration and praise, with the writers and composers:

"Holy, Holy, Holy," with words by Reginald Heber and music by John B. Dyers

"Love Divine, All Loves Excelling," Charles Wesley and John Zundel

"Come, Thou Almighty King," Author Unknown and Felice de Giardini

"O Worship the King," Robert Grant and Johann M. Hayden

"When Morning Gilds the Skies," from the German, translated by Edward Caswell, music by John Barnby

"Joyful, Joyful, We Adore Thee," Henry Van Dyke and Ludwig Beethoven

"To God Be the Glory," Fanny J. Crosby and William H. Doane

"God of Our Fathers," Daniel C. Roberts and George W. Warren

"Guide Me O Thou Great Jehovah," Peter Williams; William Williams and Thomas Hastings

"This Is My Father's World," Maltbie D. Babcock and Franklin I. Sheppard

"Fairest Lord Jesus," from the German, Seventeenth Century

"The Morning Light Is Breaking," S.F. Smith and G.J. Webb

"Crown Him with Many Crowns," Matthew Bridgers and George J. Elvey

"A Mighty Fortress Is Our God," Martin Luther, writer and composer

"Faith of Our Fathers," Frederick W. Faber and Henri F. Hemy, adapted by James G. Walton

"Come, Thou Fount of Every Blessing," Robert Robinson and John Wyeth

"O For a Thousand Tongues to Sing," Charles Wesley and Charles G. Glaser, arrangement by Lowell Mason

Even though it is unfair to compare, a personal favorite is "The Church's One Foundation," words by Samuel J. Stone, 1839-1900, and music by Samuel S. Wesley, 1810-1876. The words, as they apply to the church, are all-inclusive in describing the church and its mission.

Although "Amazing Grace," words by John Newton, 1725-1807, and music attributed to "An Early American Melody," and "Just As I Am," words by Charlotte Elliot, 1789-1871, and music by William B. Bradbury, 1816-1868, are not usually chosen for opening hymns, no book concerning ministering would be complete without including them. They truly touch the soul!

"The Doxology," words by Thomas Ken and music from the Genevan Put Psalter, is a powerful message for use in many places during the service: opening, the offertory, and closing — anytime, anywhere.

I love the old hymns of the church. They are so majestic and uplifting.

Preludes, offertory music, and postludes, which often include traditional hymns of the church, are inspiring, as are anthems and other special presentations by choirs, individuals, duets, quartets, and other grouping of persons and voices.

Hymnals are available in bookstores, as well as books about hymns and their history.

What a blessing to live in America where we are free to attend any church that we choose! We are also free to enjoy all the marvelous gifts of the church, including the music.

Music has led many to Him. Whatever leads a person to Him is a great earthly gift.

A personal note: When I was in the sixth grade, during a time when no one was concerned about separation of church and state, our teacher allowed us to have a program during the final minutes of school on Friday afternoon. By choice — and sometimes by request — I sang, in "my own amateurish way," some of my favorite hymns: "Take Time to Be Holy," "Trust and Obey," "The Old Rugged Cross," "Have Thine Own Way," and others. There are perhaps many other students who remember our Friday afternoon program because almost all the students participated.

We continue to sing these hymns in our church, and our organist and pianist often play them as a prelude, or during some other part of the service.

Chapter Nine
Every Hymn: A Message

Every hymn is a sermon, prayer, true story, song of praise and thanksgiving - or a combination of these — but always a wonderful, inspiring thought or message.

I enjoy a minister's reading some of the words of a hymn before we sing. I like to hear him emphasize the meaning and the words of the song. Hymns are a joyful, inspiring part of the service.

Like the sermon, hymns go home with us; and we often hum, sing, or whistle them during the week.

Pastors work with music directors and choirs in selecting hymns to complement the sermon topics. So much of life is built around themes and things that "go together." When one preaches about the Cross, it is only natural to go to one's memory, as well as the subject index or table of contents of the hymnal, to select hymns about the Cross. When subjects of faith and love are used, one can follow the same procedure, of course.

Coordinating and relating the music require much work and planning — including the pastor, choir, choir director, organist, pianist, and the person who prepares the bulletin.

Often, too, the members of the congregation have favorite hymns. If the church has a suggestion box, a pastor can encourage the people to write the name of a favorite hymn, or hymns. If many suggestions accumulate, the congregation and choir may choose to sing one stanza of several hymns.

Sometimes, if I arrive early for church, I look through the hymnal, and I often think: "I wish we would sing that hymn sometime."

Someone commented that her church sings the same hymns "over and over."

The selection of hymns is a significant responsibility. Like the topics and words of sermons and prayers, hymns fill varying needs of God's people.

All work of the church requires planning and preparing. The music, too, is an all-important part of the worship service: It is a blessing to all — including those who help to plan, those who choose to participate — or those who simply prefer to listen and enjoy.

Chapter Ten

ACTIVITIES THAT INSPIRE

We are taught that one should never overuse the pronoun *I*, but I hope that you will agree that the essence of this chapter requires the use of this word.

The following church experiences are very meaningful to me:

When a pastor chooses to kneel in the pulpit for the morning prayer. Our current pastor does this. In his prayer, he calls the names of those who are sick and have requested prayer. He always prays for our nation.

When the people go quietly and reverently during the altar call to kneel and pray, or for whatever other good purpose they choose to go to the altar. The memory remains always.

When the pastor extends the altar call — and then kneels to pray with those who have chosen to come forward

When the organist plays a hymn softly as the pastor prays with those who are kneeling - and continues the music as they return to their seats for the closing prayer

When the pastor returns to the front of the communion table (following the altar call) and says: "Let us pray." Then he turns toward the communion table, and thus toward the altar, and kneels to pray for "this church and its people" and for their safety, peace, and continuing faith throughout the coming week. I believe that many remember his words during the week. A former pastor knelt at the altar, also. Even as this former pastor became older, he continued to kneel. I believe that he was able to do this because his knees were conditioned toward kneeling — at church, in his study, at home, at the hospital, and in many other places.

When listening to the musical prelude, the offertory music, the offertory prayers, the opening anthem, the choir, the solos, duets, quartets, the children's singing, the interim soft music such as during communion, the postlude, and any other notes that are sounded or words that are sung

When I see people gathering to worship

Much is spoken and written about the need for public worship and "assembling ourselves together" for worship (see Hebrews 10:25). Doing so pleases all of Heaven, surely, and brings many blessing and joys to those who choose to worship with others. The grand old hymn, "Blest Be the Tie," by John Fawcett, from Hans G. Nageli, arranged by Lowell Mason, expresses beautifully the feeling of group worship: "The fellowship of kindred minds is like to that above."

I cannot believe that I was born free in America, and that I have the physical and emotional abilities to enjoy, and to participate in, so many wonderful gifts of this great country, including the freedom to love God and to worship Him — and to worship with others. I am thankful for pastors and other Christian friends. I try to thank Him often, but I pray for a more grateful heart.

Chapter Eleven

REMEMBERING SERMONS

One memorable method that I recall from more than thirty years of uninterrupted sermons, and on into the years, is the use of acrostics by several of my pastors. As you know, this method is the use of each letter of a word to represent a thought.

In June, 1992, I was asked to give the commencement address at Spaulding Elementary School in Spring Hope, North Carolina. I had worked there for five years. The children called me the library teacher, and indeed I was, because every class and student in that school came to the library for fifty minutes each week. I used part of the period to teach and part to help them select books.

Remembering the use of acrostics by my pastors, I chose to use an acrostic for the word *love* for that commencement "speech."

L for love itself

O for others

V for vision

E for eternal

The "talk" lasted about eight minutes.

This reminds me: As you know, and as you have been taught, a pastor does not need to try to preach a long sermon "to earn his compensation." He does many, many other things each day, each week!

Most people enjoy brief, meaningful sermons. (I have not done a survey concerning this idea, but sometimes, I rely on common sense. This is one of those times.)

I turn now to notes I made of sermons by the Reverend Stephen A. Smith, of Beulaville, North Carolina, a former pastor, who almost always used the acrostic. At the spring revival in our church in 1967, he used the following:

Becoming a Christian involves
Change
Choice
Challenge

In a sermon concerning sin, he used the following:
Substitute
Prayer for prejudice
Effort for envy
Service for selfishness
Love for lust
Faith for fear

Both Preacher Smith and his wonderful wife, Bertha, who, like him, was an excellent Sunday school teacher, are now deceased. As you use his idea to create your own messages, part of Preacher Smith's mind, methods, and spirit will live on.

Another choice is to use familiar sets of letters or symbols to represent ideas. I do not recall the source of these steps to salvation that I often share.

A   Accept
B   Believe
C   Confess

Another effective sermon tool is the use of a question. I recall a baccalaureate sermon in the 1950s at Snow Hill High School, Snow Hill, North Carolina, where I was teaching English and French. Dr. W. Burkette Raper, then president, but now President Emeritus, of Mount Olive College, Mount Olive, North Carolina, chose as his topic the question: *Does God Know Your Name?* He emphasized that God knows each of us by name. Then he asked the question: But does God know your name because you have sought Him and His way and have worked in His vineyard? I shall always remember the impact of that question on my life. Surely, the question and the comments had great meaning to the many students in that large class, also.

Chapter Twelve

VISITING A CHURCH BEFORE PASTORING

Whenever possible, many ministers prefer to visit a church before accepting work as pastor. Also, often a church prefers that a minister deliver a sermon when he visits. This method of becoming acquainted is a *plus* for both the minister and the congregation.

Regarding this special visit, an experienced minister spoke of organizing, planning, and praying. He emphasized that this is a time to speak naturally, according to one's true nature, methods, and personality. He stressed that simplicity is of essence so that the minister can remember his sermon easily — and so that he can speak slowly and effectively. "You have a message," he said. "Speak so that people will understand and remember."

Ministers speak under the inspiration of the Holy Spirit, but each minister must do his part by praying and planning, as the minister suggested. Benjamin Franklin wrote: "Heaven helps those who help themselves."

Further suggestions concerning a visiting pastor included the following:

> A Bible teacher recommended that "one consider waiting until later to tell about oneself, especially the parts of one's life before becoming a Christian or before being called into the ministry. A minister can share this information in a later sermon, maybe, if one feels led to do so. Perhaps the person who introduces will chose to share information about the minister's current life and his experience as a minister. When preaching a first sermon, think God, Jesus, Holy Spirit, Bible."

A class member suggested that a visiting minister consider recognizing and complimenting, briefly, the church building, the grounds, and other buildings and facilities. The new-to-him congregation, with God, has worked very hard to bring the church and all of its facilities to their current state. Letting those present know that he is aware and that he rejoices with them in their accomplishments is a pleasant choice. A natural choice of a visiting minister is to thank the church for the joy of the visit and the privilege of speaking.

There are many marvelous Christian attributes. An attitude of gratitude is one of them — in the beginning and throughout one's ministry.

When I was very young, it was customary for church people to invite their pastor for lunch. Often, a pastor drove a rather long way and stayed for the evening service. I remember so well how wonderful it was to have pastors in our home. They were always so good and gracious. They always praised my mother's cooking, especially her chocolate cakes and fried chicken. (There are a few ministers still living who can verify these visits — as well as their praises for my mother's cooking!)

Chapter Thirteen

PRAYING FOR OUR NATION

Through the years, my pastors have always prayed for our nation — during times of peace, as well during times of war: the War in Iraq, Desert Storm, Somalia, Vietnam, Korea, and World War II — and during other times of crisis. (I was not living during World War I, but I heard others speak often about that war.)

I remember well the prayers in the churches — and everywhere — during World War II. When America entered the war after the bombing of Pearl Harbor on December 7, 1941, I was ten years old. I was old enough to know that our nation was at war, but not old enough to understand very much about the war — the why-of-it, the deaths, bombings, lost ships and planes and people, the devastation in other nations, and many other horrors; yet, I understood enough to be terrified. (I believe that living during several wars helped me to help my students during the thirty-five years that I was a teacher.)

A father always prayed for his young son during family prayers. He chose words similar to these: "And help Jonathan to grow up to be a fine, Christian young man." After Jonathan became older, the father decided that he would no longer include this verbal prayer. The first night after the omission, Jonathan looked at his dad and said: "Dad, you didn't pray for me tonight."

The father asked whether he would like for him to continue the prayer.

Jonathan replied: "As long as I live here, Dad — and after I am gone, too."

This example expresses the way that I feel about our country. I hope that pastors — and all of us — will continue to pray for this country as long as I live here — and after I have gone.

As many neighbors, friends, and family will verify, in each of his public prayers, my dad, though not a minister, always prayed for our nation, its people, leaders, and armed forces and their leaders. I have never forgotten the sound of his voice and his words as he prayed for our country.

(I need to share this: I often refer to my dad and mother in this book, as you notice. Just as you, too, love and honor your parents, I feel led to share truths about my parents along the way — truths that seem to apply to something that I am writing at the moment. Thank you for accepting my references to them.)

Pastors teach their people about the power of prayer in all things, in good times and bad, in happy times and sad. They teach the importance of one person who prays. A pastor emphasized that one person can make a difference in a church, home, school, family, community, and nation. A pastor who prays for our nation not only reaches the heart of God, but also teaches his people to pray for our nation and other nations.

The Bible is filled with people — individuals and groups — who made a difference. A bumper sticker stated: One person can make a difference. Think Jesus.

America has several days related to patriotism and love-of-country: Veteran's Day, Memorial Day, D-Day, the Fourth of July or Independence Day, Flag Day, Constitution Day, and others. Many congregations sing "America," "America the Beautiful," "The Battle Hymn of the Republic," and other patriotic songs during services on these days. Patriotic poems and readings are readily available. These and other choices inspire children and young people — and all of us — toward respect for, and love of, our country.

Throughout our land, on these special days and other days, churches remember men and women in uniform and thank them for their sacrifices and services wherever they now serve, or have served, and will serve. Veterans, too, are remembered with praise and gratitude, as are all the fallen heroes of America's wars.

Chapter Fourteen

Teaching People to Be Good

A young son, who had just come home from Sunday school, was misbehaving. His mother reprimanded him by saying, "You know that you should not do that. Didn't you just go to Sunday school?"

The little boy looked at his mother and said, "Yes, Mama, I went to Sunday school, but I didn't learn how to be good."

A great challenge of pastors and teachers is to apply, or relate, sermons and teachings. This is done by stories, illustrations, examples, and comments from real life blended with the Scripture and the sermon or message. A summary at the end of the message is powerful. Pastors and teachers teach their people *how* to be good: They teach them *to be* good.

Of course, persons sharing the spiritual can always express in specific terms that which is right, wrong, good, or unacceptable, just as parents often do, without stories, Scripture, or illustrations.

I remember how my pastors, through all the years, have applied sermons and Scripture to reality and practical Christian living.

The Reverend Stephen A. Smith used to say at the end of each sermon: "Take what you have heard, separate the wheat from the chaff, hold fast to any good that you have heard, and use it to become a better person, a better neighbor, and a better follower of the Master. That you will do this is my prayer."

Like those in families and schools, pastors, as well as Sunday school teachers, assistant pastors, youth leaders, and all others involved in church leadership, teach by precepts (rules of action and conduct) and example (the way we are and what we do).

Pastors preach Jesus born, teaching, preaching, healing, doing good; crucified, arisen, ascended, and awaiting our coming at the right hand of His Father. Pastors preach about God, Heaven, and the Holy Spirit. They teach the Bible. They also teach people how to be good. Goodness is a fruit of the spirit (see Galatians 5:22 KJV).

GROWING

Chapter Fifteen

HELPING THOSE CALLED INTO THE MINISTRY

When I asked for suggestions for those who are called into the ministry, these are the ideas that were submitted:

Read the sermons of the ages by the great men of the pulpit.

Visit churches to worship with various congregations. Sometimes, when a person is called into the ministry, he will spend all his Sundays at his home church, listening to the same pastor, assistant pastor, and Sunday school teachers, as well as the same choirs and other groups. Learning from these groups is good, but when one thinks about this choice in-depth, he realizes that one learns much about methods and materials from a variety of individuals. (A requirement to observe teachers and classes worked very well during the time that I was studying to become a teacher. The hands-on experience of teaching, as the plan was called, was a *plus*.)

This suggestion is similar: Whether a person called into the ministry chooses to attend a class or college, listening to other sermons beyond the home church, and visiting other churches, certainly seem to be wise choices. We cannot live long enough to learn, alone, all that we need to know. Along the way, we must learn all we can from others. Consider making reference notes, regularly, about people, places, and events. Include dates of the event, thoughts, ideas, and inspirations. (Have you ever thought of a really good idea at night, but you were unable to remember the idea the next morning?)

Consider attending seminars, conventions, college classes, church study courses, and any other choices that will help you to grow spiritually, emotionally, mentally, and socially. (One person wrote that, in life, we need all the good influences that we can "muster.")

Consider the wealth of information available in bookstores, in libraries, and in the home: the Bible, hundreds of reference books, including encyclopedias, and volumes of other learning materials in every area of knowledge.

Consider browsing in a bookstore, a public library, or a college library. Many inspirations and much information await! Many books are available in the field of theology and religion. (I remember how fascinated I was by the hundreds of volumes available in Bible bookstores.)

Consider a book title when someone very close to you asks for a suggestion for a birthday gift or a Christmas present.

Consider using money that you receive as a gift to buy a basic book that will help you in your ministry.

Consider attending college, if possible, to study religion, theology, and church history as well as courses concerned with a wide variety of information and knowledge. One can never realize the value of something that one has learned, read, or experienced, until one day, perhaps suddenly, one can use the information to help someone to find God, His Son, and His Holy Spirit.

When Pastor Hamm read this chapter in the manuscript, he wrote: "A minister never stops learning. If he does, the ministry stops growing."

Chapter Sixteen

ON BEING SINCERELY WRONG

Over thousands of years, ministers have preached millions of memorable, unforgettable sermons. I remember a sermon about Paul. The minister said: "When Paul persecuted the Christians before his conversion on the road to Damascus, Paul was sincere, but he was sincerely wrong."

How that idea has stayed with me! How often I have been sincere, but sincerely wrong — in my decisions, choices, actions, and thoughts.

I remember an especially-humbling experience in graduate school in a course concerned with the education of the mentally challenged. On the exam, the teacher asked what one could expect from these special students when they grow up.

I wrote the best academic answer that I knew. I thought I had answered the question acceptably.

When the papers were returned, I had barely passed.

After class, I asked the teacher how I should have answered that particular question.

She said: "You should have written that they will grow up, they will get married, and they will need jobs. Something like that."

I had answered the question from the wrong point of view. I was sincere, but I was sincerely wrong.

But there is another dimension to this true story. At nine o'clock, when I returned to the car in the parking lot, I unlocked the doors, laid my books on the back seat, climbed into the driver's seat, and locked the doors. I laid my arms, folded, against the steering wheel. As my face fell against my arms, I wept as hard as I have ever wept.

I wept, not because of the low grade. As I had walked to the car, I had thought: "How many other things have I done in life such as teaching a Sunday school class or playing the organ or piano at church, at a wedding, or a funeral — and in other areas of my life — when I had felt afterwards that I had done well, all right, or acceptably, when in reality, I had failed miserably and had done poorly?"

I try to be sincere, but sometimes, I am sincerely wrong.

Chapter Seventeen

Concerning Education

Knowledge is a miracle and a mystery. We know much; yet, compared to all the knowledge available, we know only a small portion.

Generally, almost everyone has a yearning, a calling to do a certain kind of work. It has to do with genes, inclinations, talents, feelings, and influences: It has to do with God!

Many are natured to do a certain kind of work or to provide a certain service in one of thousands of jobs available. Of course, a person may have inclinations and talents in more than one area of work or service.

Many jobs and services are enhanced by, or require, educational experiences.

So it is with the ministry. Meditation, study of the Scriptures, reading, and inspiration are good, excellent, right, and wonderful, but one will agree, surely, that any educational experience, information, or knowledge that one can obtain is a *plus*, a great advantage.

Everything that we see, read, or experience becomes a part of us.

Over the years, almost all my pastors have had formal educational experiences beyond high school. Through the years, several pastors attended a college.

To each person, his or her own way. But generally, our spirit, mind, and heart help us to know that all of us need all the training, experience, and education possible for whatever work we are called to do.

Not only courses in theology, but also studies in history, literature, philosophy, and psychology, as well as in any other area of knowledge, add to one's ability to think, plan, preach, and share as one serves God — as a pastor or as a layperson. Going the extra mile, going beyond the call of duty, and putting one's best foot forward are similar thoughts.

The hymn, "Give of Your Best to the Master," by a writer with initials H.B.G, and music by Mrs. Charles Barnard, expresses a similar idea, as do many other hymns. Perhaps 2 Timothy 2:15 expresses best the purpose of an education: "Study to shew thyself approved unto God, a workman that needeth not to be ashamed, rightly dividing the word of truth" (KJV).

Let us consider the following when seeking education and when encouraging others to do so: Education expands, empowers, enables, endows, and enlightens.

Chapter Eighteen

LEARNING FROM OTHERS

Ministers are called by God to preach salvation to all mankind and to render service to people on earth. They are not called to perfection, but all of us can grow in His grace and knowledge.

As one grows through studying, praying, reading, thinking, observing, meditating, and communing, one can also grow in accomplishing the best presentation through an awareness of language. All kinds of tapes and videos are available. I keep my car radio tuned to a station that broadcasts religious music, sermons, and inspiring spiritual material so that the program is available as soon as I turn the key.

Good judgment leads in screening all books, programs, and materials.

Listening to others is another way. Just being aware of words and pronunciation is helpful. A very good speaker was asked how she learned to speak so well. Her answer: "I listen to others. I learn from them."

She added: "Slowing down and taking time to say words will surely help in speaking. The pronunciation of certain words presents a challenge. Finding correct pronunciation of words in dictionaries helps. Word pronunciation is not the most important thing, but at all times, and in all ways, we want to use the best language we know in serving the Master."

Then she shared: "The sound and pronunciation should not be artificial and formal, but simple and clear, and as accurate as one knows."

We learn from others. Reading the prayers and sermons of others is a good habit to consider. The Bible is filled with sermons and prayers: So are books. As a pastor prays, preaches, and ministers, words that he has heard and read flow naturally into his own choices and inspirations.

The Bible has always been my greatest influence in writing as well as thought. I was reared with the King James Version of the Bible as the main choice for most of the people that I knew. The King James Version still sounds "more like Bible to me," though I certainly accept the choices of others who may prefer another version.

From the Bible I learned the beauty of cataloguing: "But the fruit of the Spirit is love, joy, peace, longsuffering, gentleness, goodness, and faith... Meekness, temperance: against such there is no law" (Galatians 5:22-23). Carl Sandburg used much cataloguing in his poetry.

Ministers often use cataloguing in sermons. They also use it in summarizing at the end of the sermon.

We learn from others — what they have written, spoken, and shared.

Chapter Nineteen

STEWARDSHIP AND TEMPERANCE

Like *The International Sunday School Lesson* series, which includes a temperance lesson, my pastors, from time to time, chose stewardship, temperance, or a related topic for a study course, prayer meeting, or message.

A pastor emphasized that stewardship and temperance go hand-in-hand and that stewardship involves care and concern for all that God has given to His people, His earth, His creatures — and for all other parts and pieces of His wonderful world.

I remember finding in an old cabinet drawer a small piece of paper on which my dad had written these words: "Today I walked in my fields, and the land seemed to say to me: 'Take care of the land, and the land will take care of you.'"

Stewardship involves the care of the land, our homes, families, income, health, woodlands, churches, highways, byways, and everything that our eyes see, wherever we live, wherever we go. We were taught that the roads we travel and the places and spaces that we rent or visit, as well as the places where we shop or dine, are responsibilities in stewardship.

From Sunday school teachers, pastors, and parents, we learned the necessity of taking care of the body, guarding one's tongue, and guiding one's thoughts, as well as nourishing all those Christian attributes which make us what we are in His name.

We learned that temperance involves awareness of the good of all things: moderation, restraint, and concentration; self-discipline, self-control, and self-awareness; prayer, dedication, and devotion to Christian principles, as well as many other choices and disciplines.

We learned that intemperance included anything that we do to hurt our body, mind, or spirit. We were also reminded that in many situations, abstinence is the best — the *only* — choice, strengthened by the thought, "Just don't go there!" — in actions, thoughts, and words.

We were taught that anytime we fail to take care of what is entrusted to us, we are failing in our stewardship.

Our pastors, teachers, parents, and others emphasized over the years that life is a journey in habits, choices, decisions, actions, reactions, and consequences; that life is a matter of programming; and that life is a matter of praying, thinking, and studying to receive inspiration, guidance, and strength in all things toward discipline, moderation, and temperance.

Sometimes, in all of life, two ideas, such as stewardship and temperance, walk hand-in-hand to enhance each other, just like the joy of the Christian journey when walked with a friend.

AN ATTITUDE
OF GRATITUDE

Chapter Twenty

GRATITUDE ALONG THE WAY

Over the years, my pastors have expressed gratitude to the church and to individuals. They have all been good, gracious, and giving.

An aged woman who lived through the Civil War, and who was almost one hundred years old, was asked what she believed to be her greatest prayer.

Without hesitating, she said: "It is three words: 'Thank you, Lord.'"

When we think about these words, we can agree, surely.

Gratitude is a beautiful attribute. Expressions of thanks and appreciation enhance every life and every experience. Churches and congregations flourish from expressions of recognition and appreciation.

Churches are made up of workers as well as worshipers. Expressions of appreciation to those who serve are appropriate and appreciated:

> To any group — the Sunday school, a Sunday-school class, a young people's group, the woman's auxiliary, the men's organizations (and whatever the groups in your church are called)
>
> To the church for any special programs, get-togethers, fundraisings, and other groups or events
>
> To those who place flowers in the church
>
> To those who serve the church: the Board of Directors, the finance committee and other committees, deacons, ushers, Sunday school teachers, Bible school teachers, nursery staff, those who mow the lawn and trim the hedges, those who help

to clean or care for the church, (if this service is applicable), and other similar services. Each pastor will have committees with similar names and responsibilities.

It is always meaningful when a pastor says to his congregation at an appropriate time: "Thank you for choosing me to be your pastor."

It is always meaningful when a pastor thanks the members of the congregation for its monetary contributions to God through the church. This needs to be done only once "during his journey," perhaps, though a special fundraising or monetary project may merit special thanks, as mentioned above. The church blesses many individuals and groups and provides many services beyond the pastor's salary: So the pastor is not thanking the church for his benefits only, but for the whole mass of gifts and services to mankind.

It is always meaningful when a pastor thanks the members of his congregation for their sacrifices and services in the many dimensions of the church. (Some may question whether the word *sacrifice* is appropriate when referring to the work, efforts, or contributions to a church, but in our human way of thinking, we know that many put forth extra effort and do much planning and budgeting to help support the church and its mission. We leave the interpretation of sacrifice to God, as we choose to leave to Him the labeling and interpretation of so many things.)

Gratitude that comes naturally to all pastors is to welcome visitors and to express appreciation to them for choosing to worship with his congregation and him.

All of the above can be expressed individually, at a chosen time, in one or two sentences. Time is so important. There is so much to be remembered and included.

Pastors are talented in programming themselves toward brevity. They have only a few minutes to do many good things, including delivering a wonderful, inspiring sermon.

Pastors should feel good after reading this chapter because they can say: "I already do all these things." But listing them, in praise and gratitude, is the motive for this chapter. Sometimes a minister is asked to express his philosophy in a few words. What does one say? "I love

God above all else." ... "I pray much." ... " I cling to faith." ... " I believe." ... "I try to do the best I can always." ... "I love my people." ... " I love God above all and my neighbor as myself." ... Maybe a combination of these is an answer. Maybe the words of the old, old Civil War survivor are appropriate: "Thank you, Lord."

RELATING AND BONDING

Chapter Twenty-One

THE POWER OF LISTENING

When I was a young teacher, representatives from each school in the county were asked to attend a workshop on the subject of listening.

I wondered: "What is there about listening to justify a workshop?"

I do not remember the specifics of the workshop — though I listened carefully — but I do know that I have never forgotten the importance and power of listening.

Pastors are good listeners. They listen with their eyes, facial expressions, and body language. They listen with their hearts.

A pastor was scheduled to counsel a very troubled person. When the pastor returned home from the counseling session in the church office, his wife asked him whether he felt that he had helped. Her husband replied: "Well, he smiled and thanked me — and he seemed to go home in better spirits."

"What do you mean?" his wife asked.

"Well, I did not say or do anything. I just listened."

This thought is obvious: Maybe listening is often an appropriate answer, a good answer.

Through the years, when I went to see my parents, they always asked whether I wanted something from the garden, freezer, or farm. Sometimes I would say, "No, thank you. Today, I just want to talk, if you have time."

They always listened. I always came home a better person.

Pastors are like this, too. They listen.

After reading this manuscript, Pastor Hamm wrote: "Listening is such a wonderful example — and extension — of God's nature toward His people: God listens."

Chapter Twenty-Two

NO ACCOMPANYING SENTENCES

Thoughts that need no accompanying sentences:

The importance of

Listening to people, really hearing what they are saying

Listening to their expressions of love

Listening to their joys and triumphs

Listening for their cry from pain of body and spirit

Listening for their cry for help

Listening to their words of suffering and hearing their sadness

Listening beyond their words to hear their cry for a listening soul that cares

Listening to the words of their heart to hear the hurt that may hinder

Listening to the yearnings of their soul as they seek God

Listening without feeling the necessity to respond with words

Listening by looking into their eyes so that they can see trust and caring

Listening. Just listening with heart and mind

An idea that I heard first from a pastor was that Paul had a thorn in his flesh. The pastor stated that no one knew what that thorn was, though there had been much speculation among theologians and laypersons.

I believe that almost everybody has a thorn. If a pastor cannot remove that thorn, perhaps he can help provide the medication of caring, listening, and praying.

Ministers have a great calling. They are called to lead their people to God. They are called to walk by their side, to listen, to stand by their bedside in times of sickness, and to pray for them — and with them. They are also called to lead them to richer, fuller lives in Christ Jesus and to help them to find peace in Him.

People have many needs. There are many ways that pastors can help. Some of the needs and some of the methods for helping do not even require a full sentence.

Chapter Twenty-Three

BONDING

New pastors came to our church and listened, observed, waited — and I imagine, wondered, as almost all new pastors do, surely. (I know that this is often the approach of teachers.) Pastors prayed and preached with sincerity and love. They were not trying to prove anything: They were just doing the job that God and the church had called them to do. They were doing their work quietly and simply, but with gentle enthusiasm. They seemed to be trying to learn the customs, routines, and expectations.

I was not so aware of this until I began to pen these pages: Then I remembered how they were. Ironically, they never changed much. They were there with us, helping us to do what we had always done — and yet, at times, suggesting new choices and ideas — and helping to lead in any good way that they could. In all those years about which I am writing, there was a natural flow of work and spirit, a bonding unspoken, but there!

Pastors agree that almost always bonding with individuals and congregations takes time. Sometimes, with a new congregation, there will be an event or an experience that brings instant bonding, but usually, bonding comes with the passing of time. The bonding usually comes through the spontaneous flow from spirit to spirit, from heart to heart, from life to life.

All of this comes from purity of heart and motives. Dad always said that motive is everything. In all communications and activities — and even in waiting — the motives of both people and pastor must be pure and simple — and sincere.

A pastor who had visited a member in the hospital said to his congregation at the next service: "I was so pleased to see several of you at the hospital this week. You are good people: You do good things."

Psychology teaches that people often become what we tell them that they are, especially through deserved praise and recognition, whether private or public. If a pastor tells the people of his congregation that they are good people — if he reminds them — they will become his compliment.

Everyone, or maybe I should say "almost everyone," has a trademark. I remember a doctor who used to say to his patient at the end of an office visit, "You're a good woman, Mary," or "You're a good man, Sam," or "You're a fine young person, Jim," — and he meant it! Doing this was one of his trademarks. I believe that those who were blessed to have him as doctor and to hear his words were touched and inspired.

If, in morning prayers, or in other prayers, a pastor refers to "this good church and these good people," the people will hear — and they will remember.

And I believe that God will hear — and be glad!

Chapter Twenty-Four

New Pastors and Coworkers

An important dimension of ministering is the pastor's helping his entire congregation to feel loved, appreciated, needed, and special. This cannot be done in one moment, one visit, one sermon, or one day. Growth and acceptance come from sermons, personal contacts, notes to members, calls, e-mails, comments as a pastor greets members of the congregation before and after worship services, and in many other ways.

Not only relating to individuals but also to groups is important. Suppose, for instance, a pastor knocks softly on the door of the choir room, steps just inside the room, and says to the choir: "I want you to know that all you do makes a difference in all our services and to God. I thank each of you. I thank God for you."

A pastor always attended the Sunday school council meeting and expressed similar thoughts.

Even though some of the following are similar to thoughts mentioned in other chapters, they are worthy of blending with the following:

A new pastor learns the names of those who mow the grass, clean the church, prepare and print the bulletins, play the piano and organ, direct the choir, turn on the heat and air conditioner (or check them from time to time if they are automatic), or whatever other duties apply. A pastor finds these people early in his ministry, in places along his way, and tells them how much he appreciates what they are doing for God and the church.

A new pastor asks about people who have special skills and abilities. For example, someone may be an excellent carpenter, accountant, or artist — or have one of hundreds of skills and talents.

A meaningful choice for the new pastor is to mention the talent or skill to the person and to find eventually, if possible, a place for that person and his or her special abilities. There is something about the human spirit that is lifted and helped when a person knows that someone is aware and cares. Even if there is not a place at the moment for performance or use of a person's skills, there is joy to the person and the pastor in sharing the talent.

Churches, large and small, have all kinds of plans and practices concerning the care of the church and its many dimensions. Some churches contract to individuals or companies their plant needs such as housekeeping and maintenance of grounds; but all across America, there are many church people who take care of all the needs of the church.

Pastors know the joy of an individual when a person realizes that the new pastor knows his name and is aware that he is doing something in God's house and in His vineyard. Expressing appreciation is a gift that can be given often.

Chapter Twenty-Five

THE PR OF THE MINISTRY

Every church seems to have its challenges, at times. Even in a church, people sometimes see things differently: Things can become rather confused.

Maybe it is time for a little Christian PR — Prayer and Rest.

Another dimension of PR is waiting. Maybe the pastor and the people of the church need to pray and rest — and wait.

Years ago, on the reverse side of highway signs in North Carolina, signs giving the information, "Slippery When Wet," was written the word *think*. The word was visible to motorists when the signs were folded in non-threatening weather. My dad said that *think* was one of the most powerful words on earth.

If pastors inspire their people to pray, rest, wait, and think before acting, how many church concerns could be solved in God's way and will!

Even though we think of PR in life, in general, as referring to public relations, maybe as we apply the thought to the public relations of Christian living, perhaps we should add two letters: PRWT, for Prayer, Rest, Waiting — and before action, Thinking.

I recall, from many years ago, concerns that challenged the denomination of churches of my faith and choice. I remember how wisely all of the pastors in our area helped to direct the survival of the denomination that we had known and loved for many years. Because of their faith and leadership — and with God's help — churches in our area continued their choices in beliefs, practices, and elements of faith. I saw in their faces and being the elements of pain and strain, but they prevailed in faith, prayer, hope, and love — and the denomination triumphed.

A very effective teacher of educational methods emphasized the word *let's* in public relations — in people relations. He said that the word *let's* included the teacher and the student in learning and in making decisions. So it is with a pastor and his people.

Another idea that the teacher recommended was the use of the words *maybe we should consider*.

All of my pastors have been really good mediators. Knowledge, character, patience, discipline, and dedication — and their other Christian attributes and choices — were always obvious in all of their leadership. They passed to us the awareness and joy of compromise and peace — with God's help and always in His name.

Chapter Twenty-Six

A CAPTIVE AUDIENCE

We are sometimes a captive audience — in a group or as an individual. In school, church, weddings, families, funerals, business meetings, and other similar circumstances, we are often in groups when leaving is considered impolite or inappropriate.

As a teacher, I was aware of the concerns of young people who were expected to remain in a state-of-learning-and-listening for an hour or longer.

The challenge is to be reasonable in circumstances involving a captive audience. Pastors will agree that the ministry is no exception. I cannot write about this with full meaning because I have never had a pastor who spoke longer than the expected length of time, generally. Of course, when people go to the altar, or other such blessings become a spontaneous part of the service, the service is sometimes extended.

People express concern that they have been to funerals when the time has been extended beyond Scripture, prayers, recognition of the family with words of comfort and love, music, and words of remembrance honoring the deceased. (One reader of this manuscript shared that sometimes a family will submit information that requires a considerable length of time.)

A main concern expressed over the years concerning funerals is that a minister uses the occasion to "preach a sermon." Sometimes people say that they do not go to funerals because of the concern that there will be a long sermon in such a time of sadness. Also, people say they do not go to church because the preacher preaches too long.

To teach, preach, or speak within an anticipated time period involves thought and planning. Teachers face this challenge. So do people in television and radio.

We remember that ministers are called of God and that ministers preach under His leadership. I was taught that criticizing someone who is doing his best for God is blasphemy and that blasphemy is sin. As all of us know, blasphemy is the act of speaking impiously and irreverently about God, His Son, the Holy Spirit, the Bible, or anyone who is doing the best he can for God, whether he is a minister or a follower. Blasphemy includes cursing and reviling sacred things. Our mortality does not excuse or justify blasphemy or any other sin.

Let us remember, too, that pastors are a captive audience. They, with doctors, teachers, law enforcement personnel, and other similar professionals, are always subject to constant observation and judgment.

We are all on a great journey, pilgrims, on our way to that great celestial city of God. We are, each one, a captive audience to each other, to one another.

The idea of being a captive audience has a wonderful positive. Most of all, we are all a captive audience of God. His word teaches: "...I will never leave thee nor forsake thee" (Hebrews 13:5 KJV).

Chapter Twenty-Seven
THINGS HAPPEN

Because of organization and planning toward a sermon or service, a pastor usually has a sermon or message topic or subject, chosen Scripture, an outline, a central point or theme within the message, and a closing which includes a summary.

Sometimes it may become necessary to shorten or modify the sermon: The pastor becomes ill. A member of the congregation becomes ill. A message of tragedy, illness, or concern comes through a cell phone or personal messenger. Threatening weather, or an accident nearby, involves threatening chemicals or the possibility of fire. These and other happenings are possibilities.

Pastors must sometimes make quick decisions and adjustments during the service or the sermon. Schools, organizations, companies, businesses, families, and other groups have emergency plans. So do many churches, but usually, the pastor is the one who must make emergency decisions and announcements. You, as a pastor, will know what to do: God will help you.

One minister shared that in the quietness of his spirit, he had tried to think of possible emergencies and to visualize and plan how he would manage these situations. He realized that he might need to call on an assistant pastor, a deacon, the Sunday school superintendent, or some other adult to help. He emphasized the idea of trying to remain calm. "Remember, God is everywhere," he added.

A person who may be using drugs or alcohol may wander into the church — talking loudly and gesturing. A person with a weapon may enter and threaten.

In our church, we are blessed to have several well-trained firemen, a nurse, an emergency medical staff person, and others who can help in emergencies. Perhaps all pastors should have a meeting with all trained persons who can help with emergencies and determine a plan for an emergency.

A worship service is a world all its own. It is a community assembled. Many good things are possible. Sometimes, unfortunate, unexpected things happen. Maybe the Boy Scout motto fits here as it does in so many dimensions of life: "Be prepared." Be prepared through planning, preparation, and prayer.

Chapter Twenty-Eight

PASTORAL VISITS

A minister who read this manuscript suggested a chapter concerning pastoral visits. Later, upon request, he shared several ideas that are included in this chapter. Additional recommendations for visiting were gleaned from other sources including hospital bulletins and interviews.

Pastoral visits may involve visits in hospitals and homes, as well as visits in the church parsonage, church office, or other appropriate places.

Hospitals often recommend a visiting period in a hospital room for ten, and not more than, fifteen minutes. Of course, there are circumstances that cause the time to be adjusted. The patient, family, or medical personnel may suggest a longer or shorter stay, based on the patient's condition. It is not the length of time, but the quality of time that matters. Concern, caring, and genuineness are the mood of the moment, as all pastors know well.

With a patient's request or permission, a brief prayer is recommended.

Visiting involves hesitating or waiting in the hall, especially if the door is closed. One should never enter a hospital room without knocking gently. One should never enter a hospital room without hearing a voice inside that gives permission to enter. Personal, private necessities concerning medical care and treatment take place in hospital rooms, as every adult knows.

Visitation in Intensive Care and other similar units involves special rules. One must ask nurses, attendants, or other persons in charge about length of stay and any other information needed for communicating with the patient — or not communicating. Again, sometimes, just being there and a quietly spoken — or silent — prayer suffice.

Though repetitious, from reading, interviewing, and observing, these are suggestions for hospital visits:

Knock gently and wait for a voice to respond with permission-to-enter before entering.

Enter slowly and quietly.

Speak slowly, softly, and sincerely regardless of the patient's condition. Doing this is a choice of "one size fits all." A minister suggested "that a visitor adjust the tone and volume of the voice to the comfort of the patient."

If the patient seems to be doing well and gives the visitor a behavior-to-mirror, one can move into quiet enthusiasm, but never into a noisy choice.

Do not sit on the bed or move it, or lean against it, in any way.

Do not discuss the patient's illness unless the patient insists on sharing. Then listen with care and loving concern, but do not ask questions or make suggestions.

Do not bring food, chewing gum, colas, or other drinks into the room without permission from a member of the hospital staff because patients with certain health challenges may not be able to eat or swallow — or they may not be allowed to have food.

Do not visit if you have a cold, sore throat, or any other illness or symptoms of illness.

Do not discuss news and tragedies of the outside world unless the patient asks. Then be brief, presenting the news in simple form — and then moving to another subject, slowly and diplomatically.

There are other occasions involving pastoral visits: in the home, parsonage, church office, or other appropriate places. Common sense and good judgment tell us that all such visits should take place with planning, preparation, and prayer. A minister wrote this suggestion:

"Private visits with persons of the opposite gender should be in a discreet setting."

Again, good judgment tells us that pastors must be aware of complications of knocking on doors of homes by surprise. Because of current communications, arrangements and appointments can usually be scheduled.

People have needs, feelings, actions, reactions, habits, and often, problems. A pastor, like a counselor, teacher, law enforcement officer, nurse, doctor, or any other service professional must be very careful and tread lightly, often with reasonable hesitancy.

Counseling involves much listening. Often a person simply needs someone to listen to his or her problem.

A reality of life is that some people have mental and emotional health challenges. Pastors can become caught up in many kinds of confusing, disturbing, uncomfortable situations; yet a pastor cannot ignore this dimension of his service, if needed.

A minister wrote: "One must be careful in giving advice. A pastor must know that at times, a referral to a professional person is reasonable. However, someone may be offended if a pastor recommends professional help. In this situation, a pastor may need to ask a doctor, psychologist, or psychiatrist about the appropriate way to suggest such recommendations to a 'church-patient' or to a family member of the patient." The minister added, "Do all you can to help, but tread lightly and prayerfully."

God is omniscient, omnipotent, and omnipresent: all-knowing, all-powerful, and always-present. Pastors — and we who are laypersons — do not walk alone. This is one of the many great, comforting truths of salvation. We need only to ask to receive divine guidance, in counseling and guidance, or for any other need that we have.

Chapter Twenty-Nine

PEOPLE ARE IMPORTANT

From her podium, a college professor watched and listened as her graduate students, assembled for a three-hour class, chatted about many things. Finally, when it was time for the class to begin, she taught the class, as was expected, encouraging class discussions and questions.

A few minutes before the class was scheduled to end, she stopped teaching and bowed her head in silence.

Finally, looking at the class, she said: "I am going to tell you something, and I want you to remember it forever. If you forget all that I have taught you, try to remember what I am going to say to you now."

She bowed her head again.

We wondered "what on earth" this master teacher, so young and brilliant — and certified with a doctorate — was going to tell us among all the words and ideas that she knew.

Then she looked at us. There was much emotion in her face, eyes and voice, as she said, "People are important. Never forget."

Then she bowed her head again for several seconds. When she looked at us, she said again, "People are important. Never forget."

Then she said, "You may go home now."

We continued to sit, somewhat stunned.

Again she said quietly and sincerely, but with much emotion, "You may go home now, but never forget." Though it was not "quite time" for the class to end, we left the class as she had requested; but one can imagine that, surely, neither of us has forgotten that class, that teacher, or those words.

The essence of God to His Son: People are important. An essence of Jesus' message to the world: People are important. An essence of a pastor's mission: People are important. An essence of this book: People are important.

"Jesus said unto him, Thou shalt love the Lord thy God with all thy heart, and with all thy soul, and with all thy mind. This is the first and great commandment. And the second is like unto it, Thou shalt love thy neighbor as thyself. On these two commandments hang all the law and the prophets" (Matthew 22:37-40 KJV).

We recall the Great Commission which is recorded in the final verse of Matthew: "And Jesus came and spake unto them, saying, All power is given unto me in heaven and in earth. Go ye therefore, and teach all nations, baptizing them in the name of the Father, and of the Son, and of the Holy Ghost: Teaching them to observe all things whatsoever I have commanded you: and lo, I am with you alway, even unto the end of the world. Amen." (Matthew 28:18-20 KJV).

CHALLENGES

Chapter Thirty

DIFFICULT QUESTIONS THAT COME TO A PASTOR

A pastor is often asked questions that are difficult to answer: Where did God come from? Who made God? How old is God? When was the world created?

One response may be that the first four words of Genesis 1:1 are among the most powerful, most important words in the English language, because they are the answer and the only explanation that we have for many questions. The three words, *In the beginning*, have no date. The other word of the four gives the reason: *In the beginning God*. Mankind does not know what dates these words represent.

There are other questions similar to these: Why do people die? Where do people go when they die? Why do people get sick? Why are people killed in automobile accidents? Why are innocent people killed intentionally by others? Why do we have wars?

Then there are questions that are somewhat easier to answer.

What is the difference in the Old Testament and the New Testament?

Which is longer, the Old Testament or the New Testament — and why?

Who lived first – Abraham, Isaac, Jacob, Joseph, Moses — or Jesus?

As all pastors know, the Old Testament contains the story of the creation of heaven and earth and all therein, including the creation of the first man and woman, Adam and Eve. The Old Testament also tells the story of Cain, Abel, Seth, Enoch, Noah (and the flood), and Noah's descendants. The account continues with Abraham (1996-1822 BC) and the promise that God would make of him and his descendants a great nation (See Genesis, chapter 17). As we were taught in Sunday school, the Old Testament is, in addition to the above, the story of the descendants of Abraham and their leaders, including kings and prophets, the captivities of the people, their sufferings and triumphs — and especially their relationship with God.

The Old Testament closed with Malachi (397 BC). No recorded Scripture was written for the next four hundred years.

The New Testament, with general dates of AD 1 through AD 96, includes Matthew through Revelation. The New Testament begins with the genealogy of Jesus in Matthew 1, and then moves to the birth of Jesus in Matthew 1:18-25.

The New Testament includes twenty-seven books that tell the story of Jesus — His birth, teachings, ministry, betrayal, trial, death, crucifixion, resurrection, ascension, and triumph. This part of the Bible also includes the life of the twelve apostles, the life of Paul and his writings, (referred to as Epistles), and Revelation, a prophecy of biblical events yet to come.

Students are always excited to learn that the birth of Jesus marked a new way of dating historical events. In the history of the calendar, after the birth of Christ, historical events began to be labeled as AD and BC. Students are excited to learn that AD stands for *anno Domini*, meaning "the year of our Lord," or as some say "after Christ was born," and BC for "before Christ." Many do not know that grammarians and historians now use AD before the date and BC after the date. (The separation of church and state affects public school teachers' choices in sharing this information, but these can be taught in Sunday school and other church activities.)

Young people enjoy learning the organization, structure, and substance of the Bible. They are fascinated to learn its chronology and to observe its perfection-in-translation, as well as its beautiful language — in additional to the spiritual truths.

In Sunday school, Bible school, seminars, and study courses, as well as at home, helping young people to associate facts that they learn in school with facts related to Bible history seems to increase their understanding of the Bible.

For example, they want to know who lived first: Jesus or Shakespeare, George Washington, Abraham Lincoln, and others that they study in school. (An obvious thought: They sometimes do not know until someone teaches them.) The answer, of course, is that *Jesus* lived first. As all pastors know, Jesus was born at the beginning of the First Century, around AD 1, (the date depending on the historian that one chooses). Shakespeare was born in England in AD 1564, fifteen-hundred-and-sixty-four years after Christ was born. George Washington was born in AD 1732, and Abraham Lincoln in AD 1809.

Another interesting question from a young person: "Where was Jesus when the first people came to live in America — the people who were able to settle and survive?" The answer, of course, is that the first permanent settlement in America took place in Jamestown, Virginia, in AD 1607, (sixteen-hundred-and-seven years after Jesus was born and lived on earth). So Jesus was in Heaven when the first people came from Europe to live in America. He had been living in Heaven about 1607 years. (If one wants to subtract the thirty-three years that He lived on earth, He had been in Heaven about 1574 years.) An interesting idea is that the King James Version-Translation of the Bible (1611) took place during these years.

Young people seem fascinated to learn that Jesus, if He were living on earth today, would be the same age as the current year. A thought such as this may lead to a question such as "How can Jesus be that old and still be living?" Pastors know that the answer is that Jesus is now in Heaven with God — and in Heaven, people live forever.

Dates and events of history give meaning to the life of Christ without thinking of Him as lost in time and space. He lived in a place on earth called Palestine, which included Galilee, Samaria, and Judea. Jerusalem was in Judea. The Mediterranean Sea, which is so important to our world, was on the western border of Palestine when Jesus lived on earth. Many people have visited the Holy Land. They walk where Jesus walked and worked as a carpenter for thirty years. They see where He preached, taught, healed, and performed miracles for three years before His crucifixion, resurrection, and ascension at the age of thirty-three.

Surely, young people — and people of all ages — are excited when pastors and Sunday school teachers share truths that explain Jesus as the Son of God who lived on earth just as every other person blessed to be born.

Chapter Thirty-One
EXPLAINING SCRIPTURE

I remember how excited I was to learn the meaning of the lines: "Let the dead bury their dead" (Matthew 8:22 KJV). A pastor explained that Jesus was teaching that a person should be sure to take care of the young, sick, needy, old, and others who cannot take care of themselves. He explained that these should come first in one's choices — that there are others who can take care of the deceased. Perhaps this idea can be a comfort to those who cannot possibly, or reasonably, attend funerals because others are in great need.

Sometimes there are concerns that appear to be contradictions in the Bible. Again, a pastor helped his congregation and me to understand by explaining that sometimes a solution lies in its interpretation. For example, "Bear ye one another's burdens..." (Galatians 6:2 KJV), has been interpreted to mean that we should lovingly and willingly support, help, and forgive others. Galatians 6:5 states: "For every man shall bear his own burden" (KJV). This has been interpreted to mean that there are certain things that a person must/should do for himself or herself, whenever possible, especially in his chosen work, in finding God, and in serving God. Even though pastors and other Christians may assist and inspire in helping a person to find God and His Son, the final choices and decisions are the responsibility of the individual.

Chapter Thirty-Two
CONCERNS AND CHOICES

Young or older, some people do not hear well. Even sitting on the front pew or seat at a meeting, in church, or in a class does not help much, sometimes.

However, a realistic condition (according to the laws of nature and the differences in people) is that some voices are clearer and more easily understood than other voices. This truth applies to parents, teachers, pastors, public speakers, friends, and others.

A friend shared that she could understand reasonably well several people who participated in a program, but she could not understand the main speaker, even though the speaker was wearing a lapel microphone. She explained that she could not understand so well when the speaker looked down at notes.

In seeking thoughts concerning this, one person shared these words: "One consideration may be to breathe deeply and pray silently, 'Lord, help me,' and then, looking at the congregation, audience, class, or group, move on to one thing at the time, giving attention, clearly and thoughtfully, to each item that needs to be shared."

A challenge to teachers, Sunday school teachers, and pastors is to be aware and to speak as clearly as possible. The purpose of all speakers and teachers is to be heard and to be understood.

Pastors encourage their congregation to give to him, in writing, whenever possible, the names of those who are sick, in the hospital, or who, through expressed concern, request prayer. Sometimes, when names are spoken from the congregation, people want to pray for others, but they do not hear the names clearly. In his morning prayer, our current pastor says the names of those who have requested prayer. This choice seems to work well in our church. In a large congregation, having names spoken from the congregation or mentioning the names of each request may not be a reasonable choice.

A prayer request, whether verbal or written, is a Christian privilege. A greatest earthly compliment is that someone thinks that a person can reach Heaven and the heart of God and His Son through prayer. When a person asks someone to pray for him or her, that is the highest form of respect. A pastor explained that we must never say that we have prayed for someone, unless we have prayed, and that we must never say that we will pray for someone, unless we plan to do so. Among many other good things, pastors teach their people about the sacredness of the promise to pray.

Chapter Thirty-Three

One Thing I Hope a Pastor Never Faces

In the 1940s a young father, who had four young children, with only two years difference in their ages, had a few acres of timberland on a farm that he had bought from a member of the family. He was paying for it "by the year." A small part of the timber was large enough to cut, but some of the trees were still quite small.

Two of the man's brothers had similar amounts — according to their individual situations.

The church where they were members decided to embark on an extensive building program. The young farmer, who had almost no cash, gave several trees, and as much cash he could, for the church project. His brothers also gave trees and money.

As the church project progressed, the church board expanded the program and requested more trees.

The young farmer gave additional trees.

More requests came for money and trees.

The young farmer became disturbed. He asked his young daughter to write a note to the pastor of the church to say that he would not be able to donate more trees. He also asked her to state in the letter that because of his current financial situation that he might not be able to give as he would like and as he might be expected to give (or words similar to these).

Regardless of the sincerity of motive and the wording of the message, somehow, the situation "got all mixed up." At the next business meeting of the church, (held in another church because of the building program), a young man who had been called into the ministry, but who had not yet been ordained, stood and made a motion that the young farmer's name be taken from the church roll.

The young daughter was among those at the business meeting.

It seems that the young man who made the motion — and some of his friends — had interpreted the farmer's words as implying that he would no longer be able to support the church (referring to money and trees). As the saying goes, "Nothing was farther from the truth." The farmer was trying to say that he had done all he could temporarily.

Despite the note, committees of the church had continued to get in touch with the farmer about giving money and timber. He felt embarrassed and helpless. (He had asked his daughter to write the note, hoping that his situation would be understood, but instead, "things got worse," as the saying goes.)

The motion did not receive a second; however, the matter was discussed, but after discussion, the matter was dropped.

The young farmer continued to attend church and to support the church and its programs as best he could as he and his wife reared their children.

Another church decided that it would revise its list of members. Letters were sent to those who had not attended for a length of time, or for whatever other reasons. Implications of the letter were that the name of the person would be dropped from the church roll unless the matter was resolved.

This brings us to the title of this chapter. If I were a pastor, I hope that I would never be asked to drop or delete a name from a church roll — or to lead a congregation in dropping or deleting a name from a church roll.

I am aware of a church covenant, a church treatise, an affirmation of faith, and similar documents. Nevertheless, I hope that other answers can be found so that a name will not have to be taken from the church roll.

As a layperson, I like to believe that once a person walks to the front of a church, confesses his sins, accepts Christ, requests that his name become a part of a church roll or list of members, and becomes a member of a church, that he or she is forever a part of that church unless the person voluntarily decides to make a change. Hand in hand with the Great Judge, people need to decide their relationship with God and His church. We remember that people came to America seeking freedom to make such decisions. Becoming a member of the church is not so much about accepting a certain group of rules and regulations, but finding a place to find God.

Service is all-important, surely; but seeking in sincerity, and knowing forever the blessedness of that "still small voice," is an eternal gift.

If, for some reason, a person does not attend church, this is a great opportunity to show concern, compassion, and love. Again, freedom to worship in public, or not to worship, without fear of judgment, is an American privilege. Respect for the individual human soul, heart, and spirit is an important spiritual attribute and a great gift to every soul.

Monetary contributions, attendance, and a good life are worthy and right; but neither supercedes the human heart, spirit, and soul in its search for God and its yearning to be, in sincerity and truth, with pure motives, among those who are on the most important membership list on earth and in Heaven.

Sins of the world may be horrible and heinous, but all of us, both pastors and laypersons, hope there will always be answers besides expulsion, dismissal, and excommunication.

Church, like home, will continue to be a place of refuge, a place that we can go, and they will take us in, always — and never send us away.

Chapter Thirty-Four

LIKE A TEACHER

Like a teacher, a pastor associates with many individuals with many different personalities, needs, concerns, and backgrounds. People have many influences from homes, school, work, and community.

Generally, people come to worship services and participate according to their needs and choices. They sing, pray, meditate, observe, fellowship, and listen. These are normal parts of the service and the minister's routine.

However, in churches, growth and change are natural. Sometimes, these lead to differing opinions and feelings. Usually, the minister becomes the mediator, the liaison, or peacemaker if unrest occurs.

As a young teacher, after teaching for seven years, I accepted work in another school which was in its second year of consolidation of three schools. Each school had brought customs, habits, and expectations.

I was yearbook sponsor. Yearbooks had limited, specific budgets, which allowed only one hundred pages. Also, two colors on the cover were free, but an additional color was rather expensive.

During the early years of my work at the new school, the yearbook company offered a third color at no extra cost. The yearbook staff and I thought that this was a really good addition.

The school colors of one of the schools in the merger were gold and black. Innocently, the yearbook staff chose a black cover for the annual with two additional colors to appear in the center of the cover.

When the students from the other two schools heard about the black cover "like one of the schools used to have," they were all very much upset. They even threatened to leave school and march to the stoplight in protest.

The principal and I called a meeting of the seniors and explained as best we could, why the yearbook staff and I had made choices concerning the three colors. Some of the seniors seemed satisfied: Some were still concerned.

The next day, I received a letter of apology from the senior class with their signatures at the end of the letter. I still have that letter in a cabinet in my living room. I read it again just before I wrote this chapter.

The yearbook remained as it was originally planned and contracted.

Pastors will surely experience moments and periods of concern and unrest. Situations in a church, school, family, or community sometimes need explaining, adjustment, and compromise. Many situations call for prayer, patience, and waiting. Like teachers and other people in leadership roles, pastors are part of the great human family where there must be, at times, mediation with persons and meditation with God.

From the sermons, teachings, actions, and examples of my pastors, I observed and learned perseverance and patience – and many other attributes that flowed into my work as a teacher.

THE WAY WE ARE

Chapter Thirty-Five

Churches: Similar But Unique

A trite, but true, statement, is that we are all different. We have different approaches, outlooks, methods, strengths, habits, and customs.

Churches, too, have their own methods, programs, routines, and choices formed and established over many years and inspired by many pastors and members of the church, as well as through experiences and prayers.

A new pastor can talk with the former pastor and current deacons to understand better the customs and expectations of the church. Later, he can accept, adjust, and modify these according to his own personality, methods, and preferences, but always carefully, slowly, with much patience — and always with sincerity and ultimate respect. Observation, too, is a great teacher.

There are choices that each church includes regularly: There are other customs that a church may never include. For example, the people of a church may never go to the altar to kneel and pray. The people of another congregation may go to the altar regularly, or often.

Another church may have altar calls regularly. Many go to the altar to kneel and pray together at the end of the service. This is a beautiful picture. In contrast, a friend shared that the altar of the church that she had attended regularly during her youth was a rather small altar enclosed by banisters. She said that she never saw those of the congregation go to the altar, even before the banisters were added. She also shared that only those who wished to accept Christ as their Savior and become a member of the church came forward. Seldom did anyone go to the altar to rededicate his or her life.

For whatever chosen spiritual reasons, the people of a church may choose to respond verbally; yet some churches may never respond verbally.

A new pastor determines whether considering a custom or response is natural and acceptable to the nature of his new congregation. Also, a visiting minister, revivalist, interim pastor, or other speaker will want to consider the customs and expectations of the people before surprising them with changes. (Ministers speak under the inspiration of the Holy Spirit, as God leads: So the thoughts of this paragraph should be considered from several perspectives.)

Again, a reasonable choice for a new pastor is to observe and ask in order to learn the customs of the church. Some people may be shy or sensitive about verbal or active involvement. Sometimes, certain choices that involve the people "disturb the whole congregation and destroy the spirit of worship rather than enhance and help."

It is interesting that a congregation is usually united in the customs, routines, methods of worship, and responses. To try to change these may cause unrest. Worship is public: Worship is also private.

Pastors seem to have that special gift of knowing what to add to services. So much is involved with growth and progress. So much is involved with a pastor's using his talents, training, inspirations, and experiences to bless, inspire, and lead others to Christ. Again, like parents and teachers, a pastor has a marvelous, miraculous way of finding his place in peace and joy wherever he is called. This is truly the way I perceived my pastors.

Chapter Thirty-Six

CHOICES AND ACTIONS

Some churches — as well as some pastors themselves — prefer that the pastor not leave the altar except at the end of the service after the invitation has been extended, and later, to greet the people following the services. A friend shared that no pastor of the church that she had attended all her life had ever left the pulpit to walk down the aisle or sit in the communion-table chairs — or for any other reason except at the end of the service to stand in front of the congregation (usually in front of the communion table, when the invitation was given). We remember, too, that pastors are called of God and that they work, live, and preach under the inspiration of God: yet, there may need to be an adjustment of personalities with customs and expectations. To find one's place in life is a choice and a privilege. To know when to stay or chose another place or way is an act of wisdom.

Some churches like a very formal, quiet, organized service or manner of worship. Some churches, even within the same faith or denomination, prefer an active, verbal, involved service. Who is to say what is best or to be preferred? As a proper order of worship, a reasonable choice seems to be that the atmosphere and aura of the church should always be what brings the people closer to God. Almost always, customs and traditions are rather well established unless one is working within a new church.

A pastor, principal, teacher, superintendent, supervisor, CEO, or any other leader has his or her own strengths, methods, approaches, and dreams. These must not be stifled by traditions. Growth and change are natural, but there is a "psychology to it all," affected by thought, planning, prayer, and "giving things time."

Our journey as Christians is many-faceted, many-splendored. We are on earth to find God and His Son and to seek His Spirit, to worship, to care for one another, and to move toward Heaven. It is a magnificent journey. Pastors and people do not need to be upset, or in conflict, about a ritual or custom in the church.

The Trinity: God the Father, God the Son Jesus Christ, and God the Holy Spirit: These are the ties that bind. Though pastors and churches have their own choices and customs, seeking peace, harmony, and fellowship on this great journey toward the celestial is a worthy, necessary consideration.

The ministry is like teaching school. One can spend a whole life building reputation and harmony, but then, by one choice, one act, one word, a person can affect — or destroy — all that has been accomplished and thereby diminish or negate his effectiveness in a church, school, or other group. This is a normal risk, or possible consequence, of public work. Working with humility requires much faith, planning, prayer, thinking, awareness — and God.

Chapter Thirty-Seven
THE WAY WE ARE

As ministers learn in divinity school, being aware of gestures is important. Gestures and movements can enhance or distract: They can add to, or subtract from, effectiveness. Hands, especially. One reader noted that overuse of hands and arms can be distracting to some listeners — but added that some usage is effective, of course.

None of my pastors have used gestures that distracted, but others, from various groups, have spoken about this concern.

Gestures that are natural and that flow from the pastor's spirit are most effective, usually, as is true with any other speaker. Different religious faiths and customs, as well as individual personalities, help to determine gestures that a pastor uses.

As all pastors know, gestures need to be appropriate for, and acceptable to, one's congregation. Even though ministers are called by God and led by Him, there is that spiritual advantage of adjusting and adapting, reasonably, to a group of people. Think of two children in a family. One may require more verbal discipline. The other may respond to quiet reasoning. Often, congregations are like that! A challenge of a pastor is to try to understand the nature of people so that they will listen and grow and glow.

One does not want to be so much aware of gestures that doing so adversely affects good speaking and effective ministering. As you have been taught, be aware and care with a prayer. God will take care of the rest.

I remember that I used to pull the ends of my permed hair in school when I took notes or struggled with a test. One day a teacher wrote on a returned paper: "Joyce, try not to pull your hair when you think." I really appreciated her suggestion. Please believe that I never pulled my hair again.

Years ago when I was visiting my parents, Dad said, "Joyce, I don't mean to be critical, but I wonder whether you are aware of how often you say the words, *you know*? I was not aware, but I certainly was aware after that reminder.

I recall an experience as a very young Sunday-school teacher. I taught a lesson based on Matthew 18:6 "But whoso shall offend one of these little ones which believe in me, it were better that a millstone were hanged around his neck, and that he were drowned in the sea." Throughout the lesson, I said "milestone." Later, my dad reminded me that the word was *millstone*. I apologized to the class the next Sunday, of course.

And so, we go on together, each in his or her own way, trying! We make mistakes and poor choices, but if our hearts and motives are pure, God will help us and bring us to Him — if we ask and if we do our part.

Chapter Thirty-Eight
PASSING FROM THE MIDST

One of the many things that I learned from my pastors was that the Bible has an answer for all concerns and needs.

For example, people often have reasons to move their membership to another church: They move to another area. They can no longer relate spiritually to the traditions, choices, and services of the current church. They feel that they cannot worship peacefully because of something that has happened in the church. The challenge to all Christians is to do all things prayerfully — and to find a church where they can worship God in "spirit and in truth." (See John 4:24 KJV).

In 2004, there were over 6 billion people in the world and over 294 million in the United States, according to the *World Almanac*. Relating effectively with every person is not a reasonable expectation. Sometimes we need "to pass from the midst" of persons, groups, and situations — and move to another place. God is everywhere. The challenge is to find a place where one can worship God and His Son in His way and in a way that is meaningful toward spiritual growth.

What did Jesus, our perfect example in all situations, do when He was faced with those who would harm Him?

Consider these words from Luke 4:28-32 (KJV):

"28 And all they in the synagogue, when they heard these things, were filled with wrath,

29 And rose up, and thrust him out of the city, and led him unto the brow of the hill whereon their city was built, that they might cast him down headlong.

30 But he passing through the midst of them went his way.

31 And came down to Capernaum, a city of Galilee, and taught them on the sabbath day

32 And they were astonished at his doctrine: for his word was with power."

Things happen. Things change. God's word is the answer.

NOT WALKING
ALONE

Chapter Thirty-Nine
Seeking Help Through Books

Many reference books are written for ministers as well as for others seeking information related to religious or spiritual endeavors. These books are often used by laypersons, too, of course.

A Dictionary of the Bible, by William Smith, edited by F.N. and M.A. Peloubet, is among my reference books. During the War in Iraq, I read in a newspaper that a meeting was to be held in Ur. I remembered that Abraham was born in Ur and that he had lived there for seventy-five years before going to Canaan. Recently, I read again the life of Abraham in this remarkable reference.

A Bible history or a Bible commentary gives superb background information. *Halley's Bible Handbook*, by Henry H. Halley, is one of many excellent references.

A concordance is an invaluable reference for ministers and others. I always use an older copy of Cruden's *Complete Concordance of the Old and New Testaments*, by Alexander Cruden. As you know, almost all words used in the Bible are listed in a concordance, alphabetically, with all references for that word or subject. A minister can see how many references the Bible has for one word or idea. He can then find the references in the Bible to use in sermons or wherever needed.

Encyclopedias are an excellent reference for history of the Bible and related people, places, and things.

If you are interested in writing, *The Christian Writer's Manual of Style*, by Robert Hudson, General Editor, published by Zondervan, is an excellent reference with 432 pages.

Of course, no list is complete without the "Book of Books," *The Holy Bible*.

An up-to-date list of more than fifty-five reference books follows. The list was graciously and professionally prepared by Marci R. Rollins-Smart, who is currently pursuing her Master of Divinity at Campbell University Divinity School. Marci formerly worked with the office of public affairs at Mount Olive College. At the time of this publishing, she was employed at the Free Will Baptist Press, Ayden, North Carolina, as an editorial assistant. She has written the high school quarterly for the Press for several years.

Chapter Forty
REFERENCE BOOKS TO CONSIDER

Achtemeier, Paul J., general ed. *Harper's Bible Dictionary*. San Francisco: Harper and Row, 1985.

Anderson, Bernhard W., *Understanding the Old Testament*. 4th edition. Upper Saddle River, New Jersey: Prentice Hall, 1998.

Anderson, Ken. *The Ultimate A to Z Resource*. 8 vols. Nashville: Thomas Nelson, 1996.

Archer, Gleason L. *New International Encyclopedia of Bible Difficulties*. Grand Rapids, Michigan: Zondervan, 2002.

Arnold, Clinto E., general ed. *Zondervan Illustrated Bible Background Commentary*. 4 vols. Grand Rapids, Michigan: Zondervan, 2002.

Bagby, Daniel. *Crisis Ministry: A Handbook*. Macon, Georgia: Smyth and Helwys, 2002.

Barrett, C.K. Paul: *An Introduction to His Thought*. Louisville: Westminster/John Knox, 1994.

Boadt, Lawrence. *Reading the Old Testament*. New York: Paulist Press, 1984.

Boyd, Robert. *World's Bible Handbook: A Guided Tour of the Bible*. Iowa Falls, Iowa: World Bible Publishers.

Braswell, George W., Jr. *Understanding World Religions*. Nashville. Broadman and Holman, 1994.

Breuilly, Elizabeht, Joanna O'Brien, and Martin Palmer. *Religions of the World: Illustrated Guide to Origins, Beliefs, Traditions, and Festivals*. New York: Facts on File, 1997.

Buttrick, G.A., ed. *The Interpreter's Dictionary of the Bible*. Vols. 1-4. New York: Nashville: Abingdon Press, 1962. Supplementary Volume, 1976.

Cruden, Alexander. *Complete Concordance in the Old and New Testaments*. Eds. A.D. Adams, C.H. Irvin, and S.A. Waters. Grand Rapids, Michigan: Zondervan, 1955.

Dobson, Edward. *King James Bible Commentary*. Nashville: Thomas Nelson, 1999.

Douglas, J.D., general ed. *The New Commentary of the Whole Bible: Based on the Classic Commentary of Jamieson, Fausset, and Brown*. Wheaton, Illinois: Tyndale House, 1990.

Evans, William. *The Great Doctrines of the Bible*. Chicago: Moody Press, 1974.

Ewert, David. *A General Introduction to the Bible: From Ancient Tablets to Modern Translation*. Grand Rapids, Michigan: Zondervan, 1983.

Fohrer, George. *Introduction to the Old Testament*. Nashville: Abingdon, 1965.

Freedman, David Noel, ed. *Eerdman's Dictionary of the Bible*. Grand Rapids, Michigan: William B. Eerdman's Publishing Company, 2000.

..., ed. *The Anchor Bible Dictionary*. Vols. 1-6. New York: Doubleday, 1992.

Freemen, James M. *The New Manners and Customs of the Bible*. North Brunswick, New Jersey: Bridge-Logos Publishers, 1998.

Gonzalez, Justo L. *The Story of Christianity in One Volume*. Peabody, Massachusetts: Hendrickson Publishers, 1999.

Green, Joel B. and Marianne M. Thompson. *Introducing the New Testament: Its Literature and Theology*, Grand Rapids, Michigan: William B. Eerdmans, 2001.

Guthrie, Donald. *New Testament Introduction 4th Revised Edition*. Downers Grove: Intervarsity Press, 1990.

Halley, Henry H. *Halley's Bible Handbook*. Grand Rapids, Michigan: Zondervan, 1965.

Henry, Matthew. *Commentary of the Whole Bible: Genesis to Revelation*. Ed. Leslie F. Church. Grand Rapids, Michigan. Zondervan, 1961.

..., *Matthew Henry's Concise Commentary on the Whole Bible*. Nashville: Thomas Nelson, Publishers, 1997

Holman Bible Dictionary. Nashville: Broadman and Holman, 1991.

Holy Bible.

Kanel, Kristi. *A Guide to Crisis Intervention*. 2nd Edition. Pacific Grove, California: Wadsworth Group, 2003.

Keck, Leander E., ed. *The New Interpreter's Bible*. 12 vols. Nashville: Abingdon Press, 1998.

La Sor, W. S., D. Hubbard, and F. Bush. *Old Testament Survey*. Grand Rapids, Michigan: William B. Eerdmans, 1996.

Lockyer, Herbert. *All the Men of the Bible*. Grand Rapids. Michigan, Zondervan, 1996. ..., *All the Teachings of Jesus*. Peabody, Massachusetts: Hendrickson Publishers, 1999. ..., *All the Women of the Bible*. Grand Rapids, Michigan: Zondervan, 1996.

Mays, James Luther, ed. *Interpretation: A Bible Commentary for Teaching and Preaching Series*. Atlanta: John Knox Press, 1982.

McGee, J. Vernon. *Through the Bible Series*. 60 volumes. Nashville: Thomas Nelson, 1991.

Mears, Henrietta C. *What the Bible Is All About*. Ventura, California: Regal, 1998.

Metzger, Bruce M. *The Bible in Translation*. Grand Rapids, Michigan: Baker Academic: 2001.

..., and Michael D. Coogan, eds. *The Oxford Companion to the Bible*. New York: Oxford University Press, 1993.

Miller, Stephen M. *Get into the Bible*. Nashville: Thomas Nelson, 1998.

Muck, Terry. *The NIV Application Commentary*. Series. Grand Rapids, Michigan: Zondervan, 2000.

Newsome, Carol A. and Sharon H. Rings, eds. *Women's Bible Commentary*. Expanded Edition. Louisville: Westminster John Knox Press, 1998.

Richards, Lawrence O. *The Teacher's Commentary*. Colorado Springs, Colorado: Cook Communications, 1987.

Rogerson, John and Philip Davies. *The Old Testament World*. Englewood Cliffs, New Jersey: Prentice Hall, 1989.

Smith, William. *A Dictionary of the Bible*. Eds. F.N. and M.A. Peloubet. Nashville: Thomas Nelson, 1979.

Stonehouse, Ned B., F.F.Bruce, and Gordon D. Fee, eds. *The New International Commentary on the New Testament*. Grand Rapids, Michigan: William B. Eerdmans, 1987.

Stringfellow, Alan B. *Great Truths of the Bible: 48 Principles of the Christian Faith*. Tulsa, Oklahoma: Hensley Publishing, 1995.

Strong, James. *The New Strong's Concordance of the Bible*. Nashville: Thomas Nelson, 1996.

Switzer, David K. *Pastoral Care Emergencies*. Minneapolis, Minnesota: Fortress Press, 2000.

The Three-in-One Bible Reference Companion Concordance. Nashville: Thomas Nelson, 1982.

Tullock, John H. *The Old Testament Story*. 5th edition. Upper Saddle River, New Jersey: Prentice Hall, 1999.

Vine, W.E. *Vine's Expository Dictionary of the Old and New Testament Words*. Ed., F.F. Bruce. Old Tappan, New Jersey: F.H. Revell Co., 1981.

Vos, Howard, F. *Nelson's New Illustrated Bible Manners and Customs*. Nashville: Thomas Nelson, 1999.

Wiersbe, Warren W. *Wiersbe's Expository Outlines on the Old Testament*, Wheaton, Illinois: Victor Books, 1993.

Willmington, H.L. *Willmington's Guide to the Bible: A Comprehensive Bible Resource Center in One Volume*, Wheaton, Illinois: Tyndale Publishers, 1981.

Youngblood, Ronald F., general ed. *Nelson's Illustrated Bible Dictionary: Completely Revised and Updated Edition.* Nashville: Thomas Nelson, 1995.

As was stated in the preceding chapter, these references were compiled and arranged by Marci R. Rollins-Smart.

LEARNING FROM
PASTORS

Chapter Forty-One

LEARNING FROM PASTORS

Each chapter of this book shares something that I learned from my pastors; thus, this chapter is somewhat repetitious. However, the following list is a beginning: Each reader will recall, surely, additional blessings and joys received from pastors.

Through the preaching, teaching, prayers, and example of our pastors, we learn many good things:

> To love God with all our heart, mind, soul, and spirit – and with all of life
>
> To worship Him regardless of conditions and circumstances
>
> To serve Him with all our being, forever
>
> To study the Bible faithfully and seriously
>
> To seek education, information, and knowledge
>
> To organize one's life
>
> To plan so that one has time for work, service, duties, recreation — and God
>
> To think so that one can speak, act, and react reasonably
>
> To seek quietness in all things — even in the midst of noise, confusion, and stress
>
> To speak truth quietly, simply, and sincerely
>
> To allow time when solving problems
>
> To pray without ceasing, as the Bible teaches
>
> To meditate to improve thinking and to help in solving problems and

To realize the importance of just being there, in any good place, especially church — quietly, willingly, with pure motives

Also, from pastors, we learn the joy of

Finding answers through patience and prayer

Helping others

Understanding that we are saved by grace through faith

Being at peace with all people

Being free of envy, jealousy, and covetousness

Accepting ourselves as God made us – yet growing in knowledge and grace

Trying to go on, with His help, seeking answers through patience and prayer

Rejoicing in receiving and granting forgiveness and

Rejoicing in the progress of others

From our pastors we learn

That God and Christ Jesus and the Holy Spirit are personal to each of us — and that we can go to Them anywhere, anytime on this earth, and They will hear us and be with us.

That God, Christ Jesus, and the Holy Spirit are with us wherever we are, always, forever.

From our pastors we learn

The beauty of sincerity

The beauty of a grateful heart

The security of understanding God's word well enough to find peace in our faith now and toward the life to come

The joy of the reality that we are, each one, important in God's sight — as if we were the only child that He has on earth

From our pastors we learn

the necessity of concentrating — of keeping one's mind on what is going on — especially in spiritual concerns

From our pastors we learn about

the special gift of having been born in this great nation where we can love God and worship Him with peace and freedom from fear.

We learn about, and from, the greatest textbook on earth — the *Holy Bible* — as we hear our pastors read, teach, and preach. We like the way our pastors hold the Bible in their hand when they tell us about God.

Blended with what we learn from our parents, Sunday school teachers, church family, friends, neighbors, schoolteachers, extended family, and others — as well as what we learn from our pastors — we are, by God's grace, what we are.

Through all the years, many people have helped us to find God, and they have helped us to continue to follow Him.

We learned from each of you, from all of you...

We thank our pastors.

We thank each of you.

Let us pray that we shall continue to learn in His name and for His glory.

THESE I BELIEVE

These I Believe

Love — deep, abiding love, pure and simple —
is a heavenly gift and a great earthly joy.

Love grows and deepens when it is
nourished and lived in a pure heart.

Every hymn is a sermon.

One person can make a difference toward
peace or unrest, success or failure, joy or sorrow
— in a church, family, community, or place of work.

The Bible is filled with
people who made a difference.

We cannot live all of our dreams:
We must live some of them through others.

If success comes, be thankful and rejoice,
but remember the words of the war hero who
was being honored with a parade:
"Today it is me. Tomorrow it will be someone else."

Every decision affects destiny, but try not to look back.

Everywhere that I go, I look for miracles — and I find them.
Look for miracles. Expect miracles.

Find your work. It will become a great joy of your life.

Yearn for ways to make others happy — big ways, little ways.
Your spirit will lead your heart.

Keep motives pure and sincere. Motive is everything.

Now and at the end of life, the number of persons that we love
will be our essence, not the number of persons who have loved us.

The soul is that part of man that time passes to eternity.

Change is a permanent promise.

He who yearns for the good will find it.

Envy is a cancer that consumes.
Jealousy is a monster that destroys.
Covetousness is an illness that robs life of joy.
Gossip is a curse that destroys others and oneself.
Somehow, expressing concern for these choices surfaced in
almost every Sunday-school lesson that Daddy taught.

He who takes time for others and for the spiritual
will someday come to the point in life in completion
of other tasks and responsibilities.

Accept. Believe. Confess. These are ABCs of finding God,
maybe not in this order, but an essential three.

If a person questions why a person should believe in God,
consider the thought "Why not?"

One sentence of truth is a sermon.

We worry about what to say to a person who
has lost a loved one. Maybe "I'm sorry," and "I love you,"
spoken sincerely from the heart, suffice.

Even if there were no God, the teachings
of the Bible present the best way to live.

Sometimes we need to "pass from the midst"
of those who hurt us or affect our
spirits adversely. Jesus did this in Luke 4:24: 28-32.

In prayer, we make our wishes known. In the answer,
we find peace in knowing that we have done all we can by
going to the Greatest Power in Heaven and on earth.

A greatest prayer is "Thank you, Lord."

Often in life, we must pick up the broken pieces, and though
remembering what was lost, we must build on what remains.

I try never to say that I am praying for a person unless I really am.

I try never to say that I will pray for a person
unless I expect to keep this sacred promise.

I asked a pastor to explain why we should pray, if,
in *The Lord's Prayer*, we pray, "Thy will be done."
He said that as human beings, we ask in innocence and faith.
We wait for answers. Whatever the answer, we know that
we are in His will, whether the answer is yes, no, or wait awhile.
He continued: "We pray in order to keep our will in tune with
Him and His will — and to feel that we are in His will."

One of the greatest challenges in life is to try to live so
close to God that no matter what happens in life,
we can feel that we are in keeping with His will.

I asked a minister to explain illness, tragedy, suffering, and death.
He explained that we are mortals, not yet immortals in Heaven,
but that God is with us always, in all things, even death.

Words to consider: I love you. Thank you. Forgive me.
I understand. I respect you. I am sorry. I am praying for you.
I am glad about your success. I am sorry that I hurt you.
You are as close as a thought and a prayer, always.

Like the Apostle Paul, in his early years when he
persecuted the Christians, we may be sincere in what we
do or say, but we may be sincerely wrong.

We do many things in life because doing them is the
right thing to do — and for no other reason.

Almost every hymn is a prayer or contains a prayer.

Every hymn that we sing, listen to, or read is
a song of praise and love.

I have looked for angels wherever I have been,
and I have found them.

A most humbling experience in life is that someone asks us to pray
for him or her. Just thinking that another human being believes that
we can reach the heart of God is a most humbling experience.

We do not need to seek revenge or try to get even for wrongs that we
have received. God will take care of this for us. In His Word, he says:
"…Vengeance is mine; I will repay, saith the Lord" (Romans 12:19).

All work is honorable. All work touches others.
Working is doing God's work on earth.

Beyond life's reasonable needs, one is rich in
proportion to what one can do without.

As human beings, we often need to share the good
as well as the bad. Sometimes people are hesitant
because they fear bragging. When a person apologizes
for sharing, consider saying, "You are not bragging;
you are sharing. Thank you for caring enough to share."

Someone has said that people like us better if we are
not "so perfect," that is, if we are not imperfect intentionally.

We can compete with ourselves only, in most things, because
God created us as unique beings, each one, in all the earth.

Thinking determines actions — and actions determine destiny.
One of life's most important realizations is an awareness
of the power of thinking. Proverbs 23: 7 states:
"For as he thinketh in his heart, so is he." (KJV)

If one has a dream, a desire, or a magnificent obsession,
motivated by a pure heart and good motives, one will
someday find that dream or goal, or will find peace
concerning it, especially if these concern God and His people.

Sometimes we watch people — actors, speakers, athletes,
and others — and we wonder how they can perform so well.
Many attributes affect success, but I believe that often
their success can be attributed to concentration,
dedication, intensity of purpose, and serious mindfulness
and thinking concerning the "task at hand."
When we four children were young and playful on the farm,
Daddy would say: "You children stop playing and 'messing
around' so that we can get this work done."
Concentration is powerful.

If one wants to be involved more with people, community,
family, church, and similar groups, one must "set his mind on it,"
as the older folks used to say, and God will fill the spirit
with knowledge, strength, and ways to live the dream.

A friend expressed concern that the people she worked with, as
supervisor, were discouraged and felt that the work that they were
doing was not worthwhile. I suggested that she share with
them the first sentence of the following, plus the thoughts

which accompany the sentence: "Many people believe that
the soul is the only part of us that time passes to eternity, and
that the soul exists in mankind, in people. All good work touches
people, directly, or indirectly; therefore, all work is the process
through which we do Heaven's work on earth."

One of our purposes on earth is to help others
to recognize their importance as an individual human being
who has the Divine right to be on this earth, just as much
as the trees, oceans, and mountains.

One of the concerns of older age is the realization that,
though we tried and thought that our heart was full, we could not
love our work, family, church, associates, and God so much
as we do now, for love grows and strengthens each day.
We can only look back with a prayer that God will fill the voids
to let others know that we love them even more in our older years.

It does not matter who gets the credit, just so the job gets done.

If the Holy Spirit of God and His Son can reach from Heaven
into the lives of believers on earth, surely the spirit of Christian
friendship can reach across the miles with meaning and joy.

The ability to love usually comes spontaneously.
If it does not come naturally and spontaneously,
it cannot be forced, but it can be practiced — with sincerity,
if truly desired — until it becomes a true part of
one's nature and character. We have often heard
the expression, "I learned to love..."

The new becomes old and the old becomes new. Maybe "the old
becoming new" is one of the things that Heaven is all about.

If we stretch forth our hands, one to the left and
the other to the right, and we look at our body,
we see that it is the shape of a cross. A cross reminds us of the old,
rugged Cross with its symbolism of suffering and pain.

And yet, in life, no matter where we are on this earth,
when we look at the horizon, it looks as if the sky,
as if Heaven itself, is touching the earth — and so it is.

I believe in the holy birth of Jesus, His thirty years as a carpenter,
His three years as a traveling preacher and teacher; His arrest,
trial, and crucifixion; His resurrection — which was followed by
forty days on earth, including thirteen appearances during those
forty days following the resurrection — and His ascension to
Heaven where He waits for us at the right hand of God.

I believe that Jesus Christ is the Son of God and that His Spirit lives
in each of us — whether we recognize and accept His Spirit —
or not. I believe that His Spirit is in us, waiting for us to respond
— but that we must respond by accepting God and His Son, Jesus
Christ, as our Savior in order to be saved and to inherit eternal life.

I believe every word of the Holy Bible.

Ecclesiastes 1: 9-10 teaches a great truth: "The thing that hath
been, it is that which shall be; and that which is done is that
which shall be done: and there is no new thing under the sun.
Is there any thing whereof it may be said, See, this is new?
It hath been already of old time, which was before us." (KJV).

We write, think, speak, and express ideas that we have heard
or read during a lifetime, but in different words. So it is
with these sharings. Not one of them is new or original, surely,
though the thoughts are not borrowed or reworded intentionally.
The thoughts in "These I Believe" have become a part of my life,
and they have been — and still are — meaningful to me.
Sharing them is a joy from my spirit to yours. You may not
agree with all — or have similar feelings and interpretations.
We are all one; yet, we are all different. Each must find his or her
own way with God, His Son, and His Holy Spirit. Doing so is the
greatest mission in life, the greatest journey, the greatest joy!

Joyce Proctor Beaman

TO SHARE

CHRONOLOGY OF THE BIBLE

The Creation of Heaven and Earth

The Creation of Adam and Eve

The Garden of Eden

The First Sin

Adam and Eve Expelled from the Garden

Birth of Cain and Abel

Murder of Abel by Cain

Seth

Enoch

Methuselah

Noah

The Ark

The Flood

The Covenant with Noah

Abraham

Sarah

Ishmael

The Covenant with Abraham

Isaac

Jacob

Esau

Joseph

Moses

Aaron

Caleb

Joshua

The Judges, sixteen, including
Gideon, Samson, and Samuel

The United Kingdom: three kings:
Saul, David, and Solomon

The Divided Kingdoms of Judah and Israel

Judah: one dynasty (David's)

11 kings and one queen

Israel: 9 dynasties, 19 kings

(Judah about 400 years; Israel, 260 years)

(Judah only, 136 years)

The Captivity of Judah by
Nebuchadnezzar, king of Babylon:
Captured Jerusalem three times
including the

Destruction of the Temple 586 BC

Temple rebuilt: Completed 516 BC

Second return under Ezra and Nehemiah

Wall of Jerusalem rebuilt, 444 BC

Period of about 400 years between the
Old Testament and the New Testament.

Malachi, a contemporary of Nehemiah,
wrote the final book of the Old Testament
in 397 BC (four chapters).

Then for a period of
400 years, no Scripture was written.

However, the book of Malachi
contained a prophecy concerning
the birth of Christ in Malachi 3:1-2.

This prophecy, with other prophecies, came true
with the coming of Christ at the beginning
of the First Century, AD 1-100, as
recorded by Matthew and Luke in the first
books of the New Testament.

The New Testament was written
during AD 100.

Then the *Holy Bible*
that we love was finished.

(The preceding, abbreviated chronology was gleaned by the author from many sources through many years. Even though each fact is known by ministers and other persons involved in religious work, I am including the chronology in respect of the *Holy Bible* — for it is the source of inspiration to pastors who inspired this book. It is the "Book of Books" for those of the Christian faith. Many Christians enjoy knowing the events and people of the Bible, in chronological order: Doing so brings organization and unity to knowledge and understanding of God's great plan for mankind.)

Pearls of Great Price

The Lord's Prayer
Matthew 6: 9-13

The Sermon on the Mount
Matthew 5, 6, 7

The Birth of Jesus
Matthew 2:1-15
Luke 2:1-20

The Life of Jesus
Matthew   Mark
Luke   John

The Crucifixion of Jesus
Matthew 27   Luke 23
Mark 15   John 19

The Resurrection of Jesus
Matthew 28   Luke 24
Mark 16   John 20

The Ascension of Jesus
Mark 16:19
Luke 24:50-51

The Great Commission
Matthew 28:18-20

The Coming of the Holy Spirit
Acts 2:1-11

The Disciples of Christ
Matthew 10:2-4
Acts 1:13 and later Matthias
in Acts 1:26

The Conversion of Paul
Acts 9:1-31
Acts 22:3-16
Acts 26:9-21

The Parables of Jesus
Matthew Luke Mark

The Miracles of Jesus
Matthew   Luke
Mark   John

The Covenant with Abraham
Genesis 17

The Shepherd's Psalm
Psalm 23

The Way of Salvation
Romans 10:9-10
John 14:6
Matthew 16:24
John 3:16

The Great Comforter
John 14:1-3
Matthew 11:28-30

The Ten Commandments
Exodus 20
Deuteronomy 5:7-21

The Sermon on the Mount
Beatitudes
Matthew 5

The Golden Rule
Luke 6:31

The Golden Text
John 3:16

A WAY FOR PASTORS AND FOR US
Ephesians 4:1-15

1   I therefore, the prisoner of the Lord, beseech you that ye walk worthy of this vocation wherewith ye are called,

2   With all lowliness and meekness, with longsuffering, forbearing one another in love;

3   Endeavouring to keep the unity of the Spirit, in the bond of peace.

4   There is one body, and one Spirit, even as ye are called in one hope of your calling;

5   One Lord, one faith, one baptism,

6   One God and Father of all, who is above all, and through all, and in you all.

7   But unto every one of us is given grace according to the measure of the gift of Christ.

8   Wherefore he saith, When he ascended up on high, he led captivity captive, and gave gifts unto men.

9   (Now that he is ascended, what is it but that he also descended first into the lower parts of the earth?

10   He that descended is the same also that ascended far above all heavens, that he might fill all things.)

11   And he gave some, apostles; and some, prophets; and some evangelists; and some pastors and teachers;

12   For the perfecting of the saints, for the work of the ministry, for the edifying of the body of Christ:

13   Till we all come in the unity of the faith, and the knowledge of the Son of God, unto a perfect man, unto the measure of the stature of the fulness of Christ:

14 That we henceforth be no more children, tossed to and fro, and carried by every wind of doctrine, by sleight of men, and cunning craftiness, whereby they lie in wait to deceive;

15 But speaking the truth in love, may grow up into him in all things, which is the head, even Christ.

From the Epistle of Paul, the apostle, to the Ephesians, KJV, AD 64

Surely, Ephesians 4:1-15 speaks profoundly and beautifully, with marvelous instructions and guidance, to pastors — and to each of us — on our Christian journey.

ONE SOLITARY LIFE

He was born in an obscure village,
the child of a peasant woman.
He grew up in another village where He worked
in a carpenter's shop until He was thirty.
Then for three years, He became an itinerant preacher.
He never wrote a book. He never held an office.
He never had a family or owned a house. He didn't
go to college. He never visited a large city.
He never traveled two hundred miles from the place
where He was born. He did none of the things
that one usually associates with greatness.
He had no credentials but himself. He was only
thirty-three when the tide of public opinion
turned against Him. His friends ran away. He was
turned over to His enemies and went through
the mockery of a trial. He was nailed to a cross
between two thieves. While He was dying,
His executioners gambled for His robe,
the only property that He had on earth.
When He was dead, He was laid in a borrowed grave
through the pity of a friend.
Nineteen centuries have come and gone, and today,
He is still the central figure of the human race
and the leader of mankind's progress.
All the armies that ever marched, all the navies
that ever sailed, all the parliaments that ever sat,
and all the kings that ever reigned, put together,
have not affected the life of man
on this earth so much as that
ONE SOLITARY LIFE.

Author Unknown

THE MAN AT THE GATE

I said to the man at the gate of the year:

"Give me a light that I may go forth into the unknown."

And the man replied:

"Go forth and put your hand into the hand of God. That shall be to you better than a light and safer than any known way."

(A New Year's message from Great Britain's King George to his embattled people at the beginning of World War II. Also attributed to M.L. Haskins. Often used by Sir Winston Churchill.)

POSTLUDE

POSTLUDE

Thank you for letting me share this part of my life's journey. You have already used many, and perhaps most, of the ideas in this book. Yet, if just one word or thought helps or brings to memory something you may have "stored away," I hope that you will consider this material worth your consideration. As I stated in a previous chapter, having written other books, I thought that I had finished; but alas, writing those books was not the end.

To me, there is something very special about a person whom God has called into the ministry — a life, a spirit, a heart that God has spoken to, touched, and called forth to do His work on earth. I realize that God touches lives in many ways — and in special ways when people come to Him — but somehow, when I shake my pastor's hand on Sunday morning, and at other times, I feel that I am touching a very special being that God Himself has touched in a very special way.

There are many others who are called into many dimensions of Christian service: missionaries, evangelists, Bible teachers, Sunday school teachers, and others; but no one touches two young hands, with God, to join them in a lifetime relationship in the way that a pastor does: No one touches the head of a tiny babe at the moment of christening to ask God to bless and sustain until that later day of accountability: No one touches the feverish hand or forehead of the hospital patient with words of hope and comfort: No one reaches forth his hand to touch the hardwood or metal beneath a floral arrangement to speak those final, earthly words — no one, in the same way as a pastor.

When we all get to Heaven, pastors will see those whom they have helped to find their way — and the Way — as they traveled the greatest journey on earth — the journey that leads to God.

All of us are looking forward to seeing all our pastors, friends, and kinsmen. We shall want to tell them again about the great influence that they had on our life — and the difference that they made in our life. All of us are looking forward to seeing God and His Son, and feeling, in a heavenly way, the Holy Spirit.

Thank you for choosing to read this book.

Again, although God is in my other books, written or implied, this one is special to me: It is my song of gratitude to God, His Son, and His Holy Spirit, to my pastors, and to each of you.

ABOUT THE AUTHOR

Joyce Proctor Beaman, a lifelong resident of Wilson County, was a teacher in the public schools of North Carolina for thirty-five years. Church has been a part of her life for more than twice that length of time — going back to her "baby-in-a-blanket" days. Even though she is the author of five previously published hardback books, she felt that this was a book that she just had to write: When you read this book, I believe you will understand why.

9 781600 373596